MISS CHAVE'S DIARY

MISS CHAVE'S DIARY

from 1897 to 1898

Angela Hodges
15.9.22

Edited by

Angela Hodges

© Angela Hodges, 2022

Published by Angela Hodges

A CIP catalogue record for this book is available from the British Library.

ISBN 978-1-9996978-2-2

Book layout and cover design by Clare Brayshaw

Front cover illustration: *Ladies of the Wheel 1896 by François Courbain* (Wikimedia Commons)

Prepared and printed by:

York Publishing Services Ltd
64 Hallfield Road
Layerthorpe
York YO31 7ZQ

Tel: 01904 431213

Website: www.yps-publishing.co.uk

Contents

With much gratitude for all their help to:

The Chave family – particularly Thomas Bailey and Sally McLean, Will Barber Taylor, Phil Hodges, Carol Parker, Dawn Robson, Lizzie White, Sue Moore, Mary Graham, Julie Neale, Elizabeth Semper O'Keefe, Stuart Webb, Laura Housden of Cambridgeshire Archives, Rhys Griffiths from Herefordshire Archives and Records Centre, Bowden Preparatory School at Altrincham.

Preface

Florence Chave wrote this diary at the age of 30 in an exercise book which is held with the rest of the Chave family papers in the Herefordshire Archives and Records Centre (HARC).

Flo was the eldest of six children of William and Caroline Chave. William was a well-to-do, respected businessman in Hereford, one time Mayor, and owning property in Australia. Mabel, the sister closest to Flo in age, had a university degree (unusual for a woman in those days) and taught in a school. She became the Treasurer of the local Suffragist Society in Hereford after the death of her father in 1909. Mabel never married, and died at the Moor House in 1920, aged 51. At the time of the diary, brother Thomas was aged 27. He was a GP (later having a practice in Cardiff) and later became an expert radiologist. The next brother, Edward ("Dear Old Hewitt" of the diary) had taken over the running of the cider business for his father, William Chave, who suffered poor health. Pretty little Caroline ("Ivy") Chave, the youngest daughter, married Charles Prell OBE in Australia in 1896 while the Chave family were visiting the Queensland property inherited by Mr Chave. 19 year old Harold, the beloved youngest child, was also out in Australia at the time the diary begins.

It seems as if Flo is set to be the daughter who will stay at home to look after her parents, run the home for them as they grow older, and be an affectionate aunt to nephews and nieces at home and abroad. Suddenly, however, out of the blue on 1st January 1898, she writes in her diary: "Expected Dr Mac but he never came. Rather afraid my letter must have offended." Kindhearted Dr William McCutchan – poor, foreign and working in a lunatic asylum – is perhaps not the suitor the Chaves would have chosen for Flo, but in spite of her family's doubts she accepts his proposal of marriage.

The Chave Family – late 1880s.

Back row: Mr William Chave, Hewitt. *Middle row:* Tom, Mrs Caroline Chave, Florence, Mabel. *Front row:* Ivy, Harold

[Photo courtesy of Sally McLean]

July 1897 – Torquay

Flo's grandparents on both her father and mother's side were Devonshire farmers, and there were close family links in Devon. The diary opens while the Chave family are staying in Devon for the summer. Their time is divided between Torquay and the little village of Cove, just north of Tiverton, where Flo's Aunt Anna Bond lived.

Monday 26th July

A letter arrived saying we might expect Rose[1] and a friend of Willie's. I went down to the station to meet them. They got out at Torquay so I found them here on my return.

In the afternoon we had a carriage and drove round the New Cut, finishing up at Anstey's Cove where we had our tea, then walked across to Babbacombe. From there, Aunt Sophie and I rode home and the others walked.

Tuesday 27th July

Mr Bedborough, Rose and I went down the Dart and had a beautiful day. We had some time to wait at Dartmouth which we employed in seeing the town, Church and remains of the castle at Totnes. Rose and I sent our escort off to have some lunch and we partook of the sandwiches we had brought and then went to a little shop and finished up with raspberries and cream. From there we returned to Newton[2] where we parted, Rose and Mr B. going back to Cove and I returned to Torquay.

---

1   Rose Bond, aged 25 at time of diary, Flo's first cousin, daughter of Mrs Chave's sister, Anna.

2   Newton Abbott.

1

Anstey's Cove, Torquay between 1890 and 1900 –
Detroit Publishing Company [Wikipaedia]

Ladies Bathing Cove – Beacon Cove,
Torquay, a favourite with ladies during
the Victorian period. Page from
'Sketches by Richenda Cunningham at
Torquay & its neighbourhood in April &
May 1854 [Wikipaedia]

Wednesday 28th July

Had a great excitement after dinner caused by the flight of "Little Billie".[3] He flew right over into the nurseries and I found him comfortably settled on a dahlia. He returned a sadder bird and feeling very ashamed of himself. Edith Persey,[4] Aunts and I went to a Liberal Women's meeting held in the garden of an empty house.

After tea, we adjourned to the President's[5] house and she gave us a very nice address on her balcony. She was so lively looking one could not help liking her. We must have been the 'chosen of the guard' for she took us into her drawing room and showed us a real cast from Herculaneum and a picture that had been exhibited in the Royal Academy called "Daffodils". The artist took a fancy to her little girl and asked if he might paint her into it; he never afterwards lost sight of the child and when she was old enough, he married her. The picture was sold and they never expected to get it again but one day the gentleman bought it at a sale and presented it to his mother-in-law.

Thursday 29th July

Aunt Elise and I rode over to Brixham, had tea with Mrs Baddeley[6] and got home just in time to clean our cycles and meet Mother and Mabel[7] who arrived about 7, both looking very well. Father got out at Taunton and staying a while at Frank Merson's.

---

3   "Little Billie", Flo's corella – an Australian white cockatoo.

4   Edith Persey, aged 14 at time of diary, lived next door to Rose Bond in Bickleigh in 1891.

5   President of LWA at this time was Mrs Caroline Brine, well known speaker on Women's Suffrage among other topics. Caroline Brine and her husband lived in a house in Lower Erith Road, Torquay.

6   Mrs Baddeley, neé Upham, widow of John Colwell Baddeley. The Uphams had a ship building company; the Baddeleys were ship owners. Mrs Baddeley, aged 67 at time of diary, lived in New Rd, Lower Brixham.

7   Mabel Chave, Flo's sister.

Friday 30th July

We spent most of the morning in the shops, and afternoon and evening I was mostly occupied with two letters. Mabel and Aunt Sophie went to the dentist after tea or we should have gone for a ride.

Saturday 31st July

We had a dinner picnic down at the ladies' bathing cove, then Aunt Elise, Mabel and I cycled to Bovey – twelve miles each way. We left at 4, had our tea there and got home again before 8 so we thought we had done very well and enjoyed our little outing much, in spite of scorches and such like disagreeables.

Mabel Chave – Flo's younger sister, born in 1868.

Obtained a B.A. in 1892. Treasurer of the Hereford Branch of the NUWSS (National Union of Women's Suffrage Societies) – the NUWSS believed in peaceful protest. Described as "Governess – School" in 1891 census.
She died at The Moor House, Hereford, in 1920, aged 50.

Photo: Dr W A McCutchan ca 1895

August 1897

Sunday 1st August

May and I went to All Saints, the rest to Trinity in the evening. Aunt Sophie and mother to Trinity and Aunt Eliza, May and I to Upton. Mrs Sharp and her son called after evening service.

Monday 2nd August

Bank Holiday so our only dissipation was a bathe. Edith Persey came to tea afterwards. They all went over the Cockington. Alice went out so Billie and I had the house to ourselves.

Tuesday 3rd August

Mabel, Aunt and I cycled to Holne. Mother and Aunt Sophie came by train. We arrived first and met them, had our dinner at the Lodge and then strolled through the Chase until tea time when we again returned to the Lodge after which we started for home. I made a bad beginning, trying to carry a basket on my handle bar, caught my knee in it and was upset in a twinkling, bent my brake and bruised my knee, otherwise not much damaged. Got home alright, we did about 34 miles ride.

Wednesday 4th August

Had a bathe and then May and I went to town as I had a blouse to try on and took my bike to be repaired. Received some shortbread as a present. It was very nice. Did not do more rest of the day. Wrote some letters.

Thursday 5th August

Mabel, Aunt and I rode through Stoke Gabriel to Galmpton. Took tea with Miss Mogridge,[1] six people had come unexpectedly and we made nine, rather a large surprise party. It was nearly dark when we got back. We had to come pretty quickly for fear of being after time.

Friday 6th August

Rather inclined to be stormy so we gave our steeds a rest. Had a busy morning cleaning it so was not sorry to escape redoing it.

Saturday 7th August

Had a lovely picnic to Berry Castle, a picturesque old ruin. We rode. Mother and Aunt by train, coach and walking, reached there soon after ourselves. After lunch we walked about the wood which was small but very pretty, then we rode on to Colleton[2] and ordered tea at a little cottage by the wayside and waited for the pedestrians. We had our meal in a meadow close to the road. It was very public but afforded the passers by a little amusement so we did not mind. We got home in very good time so were able to groom our steeds.

Sunday 8th August

A very wet day so we had to content ourselves indoors. Willie came back in the evening.

Monday 9th August

Went for a walk in the morning with Aunt and Henry and persuaded Henry and Rose to cycle by themselves in the afternoon as I wanted to write.

Tuesday 10th August

Henry and Willie cycled to Exeter. Rose and I to Bampton and out in the morning blackberrying with Aunt Anna.

---

1   Miss Mogridge. There are four Miss Mogridges in the diary. Three sisters: Maria/ Mary ('Polly') – aged about 47 in 1897, Fanny aged 52 (married to Mr Pittard in Yeovil), and Bessie aged 49 (married to Mr King in London), plus an Ethel Mogridge (aged about 20 in 1897).

2   Colleton – possibly Collaton St Mary

Cockington Forge between 1890 and 1900 (Library of Congress) [Wikipaedia]

The romantic ruin of Berry Pomeroy Castle, to the west of Torquay, is reputed to be one of the most haunted in the British Isles – Yale Center for British Art [Wikipaedia]

Wednesday 11th August

Aunt Sophie and Mrs Walker went to Teignmouth by brake (Liberal Women's). They were not home until so late, Mr Walker had to stay the night. Father and Anna Langdon[3] arrived in the afternoon. The former we expected but were not sure about the latter. Mother and Mabel met him. I went for my finishing lesson with Mr George. He did not find much fault. In the evening we rode out to Miss Mogridge.

Thursday 12th August

Mrs Walker went in town with Mother in the morning and accompanied us to a picnic Miss Mogridge was giving us at Elbury Cove. In the afternoon we rode our cycles.

Friday 13th August

Father, Mother and Aunt Sophie[4] went to Exeter. They had such a wet day. Father came home early. I had a busy day turning out my boxes and putting them together again.

Saturday 14th August

Went to bathe before breakfast and Mother lost her wedding ring. She knew exactly when she dropped it so Mr Shears dropped a heavy stone down to mark the spot in the hopes of finding it when the tide went out. She started down again directly after breakfast and whilst she was there the man had the good luck to find it. Father had another doctor in to see him. He was reassuring I am glad to say. Carrie Langdon[5] and I went to the dentist. We spent most of the day in town getting ready and having our cycles put in order for our ride to Bristol.

---

3   Anna Langdon (38 yrs), daughter of Mrs Chave's eldest sister, Sarah who married William Langdon, Provision Dealer in Bristol. Anna's sister, Carrie, was the girl who accompanied Flo on her cycling expedition to Bristol.

4   Aunt Sophie – Sophie Stone (47 yrs) – younger sister of Flo's mother, based in Torquay with widowed sister Elise/Eliza Lang.

5   Carrie Langdon – Caroline Eliza Langdon (27 yrs) – daughter of Flo's mother's eldest sister, Sarah Stone. Carrie and her twin, Edith, were born in Wiveliscombe in 1870. Carrie's parents lived in North Road, Bristol.

Sunday 15th August

Wet morning. Does not look at all promising for our cycle expedition. Father did not go to church. The rest of us mostly went to All Saints.

FLO'S CYCLING EXPEDITION
TORQUAY TO BRISTOL
AUGUST 1897

Flo and her cousin, Carrie Langdon, cycle from Torquay to Bristol

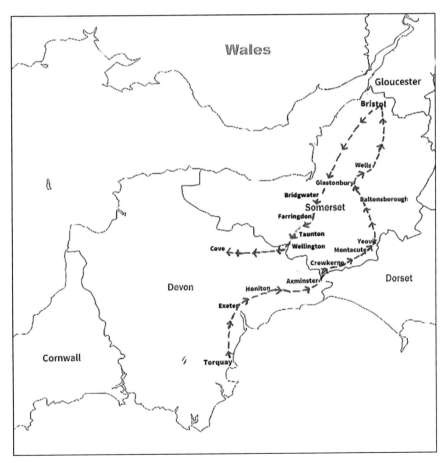

Flo's Cycling Expedition
[Lizzie White]

Monday 16th August

Rode to Exeter. Arrived 1 o'clock. Cycled out to the Tremletts[6] and had tea on the lawn, then had a children's party. Miss Luget[7] called for us and in the evening we called on Miss Burston.[8]

Tuesday 17th August

Had a swim in the baths before 6.30. Wet morning. Miss Luget rode first 11 miles with us. Hard road to Honiton. 16 miles. Refreshed there then went on to Axminster. Had another tea with Mrs Wolland[9] and refreshed again at Crewkerne. Looked very stormy in between but we were able to ride all the way and reached Yeovil 7.30 feeling we had been quite far enough.

Wednesday 18th August

Went in town in the morning and had a bathe. Paid calls in the afternoon on Mr Pittard[10] and Mr Barry/?Banfield. The latter's dog followed us all the way home so we had to walk in again with it in the evening which was tiresome as it was frightfully wet.

---

6   Tremletts – the Tremlett family lived at Villa Rouge, Spicer Rd, Exeter. Arthur (57 at time of diary), paper manufacturer. Mrs Emma Tremlett was born in Bickleigh, where Flo's cousins lived in 1891. There were two sons, Alan and Ernest (24 and 22 at time of diary).

7   Miss Luget – possibly Miss Violet Luget (24 at time of diary) Postmistress, living with younger sister, Kate at 44 Magdalen Street, Exeter in 1901.

8   Miss Burston – possibly Miss Louisa Burston, milliner at 16 South St Exeter in 1891 (36 at time of diary) with a servant and three shop girls, one of whom was an Evelyn Chave aged 24, born Halberton.

9   Mrs Wolland – possibly Mrs Rosina Wolland (41 at time of diary) lived with husband, Thomas, and daughter, Maria, in Church St, Axminster. In 1891 they were living in Silverton, nr Bickleigh.

10   Mr Pittard – Mr Charles W Pittard of Pittards' was married to Fanny Mogridge. Flo visited a Miss Mogridge near Torquay before her trip. Charles Pittard inherited a leather dressing business from his father. He married Fanny Mogridge (born Torquay) at Newton Abbot, Devon in 1868. They had seven children: The eldest, Florence, born 1869, was 2 years younger than Flo Chave. The "Mr Pittard" mentioned could have been Charles Pittard or one of his sons – Harold (aged 25) or Wreford JC Pittard (aged 20). The Pittards lived in Middle Street, Yeovil. C W Pittard was made an Alderman in 1897. He was firmly in favour of women's suffrage.

Thursday 19th August

Edith took us to Montacute and Ham Hill[11] where we had our tea and a very enjoyable afternoon, the only drawback being a race to catch the train. Fortunately, it was late or we should have missed it and had to walk all the way home.

Montacute 1890–94
Photo: Dr W A McCutchan [By kind permission of HARC]

Friday 20th August

Rode to Baltonsborough. Would have been a lovely ride, such a nice road, only we were caught in a heavy storm and as it had been raining out there all day the roads were awful. I had one sideslip but luckily came off on my feet. It was a quaint old farmhouse where we stayed, their lives being devoted to making stilton cheese. I saw as much of the process as I could and felt very thankful not to have my living to gain in that way.

---

11   Ham Hill overlooks Stoke sub Hamdon where Dr McCutchan was Medical Assistant from 1890-94. Flo was likely to have been aware of this but does not mention it in her diary.

Ham Hill Quarries 1890–94
Photo: Dr W A McCutchan [By kind permission of HARC]

High Street, Exeter between 1890 and 1900 – Library of Congress [Wikipedia]

River Avon from Clifton Downs, Bristol, between 1890 and 1900 [Wikipedia]

Saturday 21st August

Rode to Bristol through Glastonbury and Wells. Took a look at the latter Cathedral. The day was stormy but we were lucky each time in being able to shelter. Went to Aunt Sarah's to tea. Left our machines there and to Miss Tudway's[12] to sleep.

Sunday 22nd August

Stormy. Carrie went home. Morning wrote letters. Afternoon walked across the Downs and took tea with Mrs Thomas. Called for Carrie in the evening.

Monday 23rd August

Started 11.30. Reached Bridgwater 6.35. Very good road most of the way.

---

12   Miss Tudway – Miss Charlotte Tudway (aged 50 at time of diary – a poulterer living at No 2 The Mall, within walking distance of Clifton Downs. In 1891 was living in same house as Rachel Chave, born Wiveliscombe.

Called on Aunt Corner[13] and Mrs Gray. Mr Gray[14] rode out to Farringdon with us as it was quite dark and we had to have lights.

Tuesday 24th August

We could not move on as we intended doing for it was a very wet day. Mrs Merson[15] was very nice and kind to us and took us for a short drive in the evening.

Wednesday 25th August

Left at 10.15. Met Mrs Sharp[16] in Taunton. Had it very nice to Wellington where we had a nice lunch. We had a sharp shower soon after and muddy the rest of the day. We had tea at Aunt Rachael's.[17] I was sent a terrible way to Cove, such roads. Certainly not meant for a cycle to traverse. I was just on the verge of despair when I found myself at my destination about 7.30 and very nearly dark. Rose had a houseful, Father, Mother, Blanche Hitchins[18] and the two little Perseys.

Back in Cove, near Tiverton

Thursday 26th August

Was wet all day so we could not go out. Cleaning my machine was no light task.

---

13   Aunt Corner – Anne Corner neé Chave, widow of Edward Corner, Farmer. Visitor to Flo's Chave grandparents in Bampton in 1861. Lived at 10 North Fields, Bridgwater.

14   Mr Gray – (aged 40 at time of diary) lived at 15 Cornhill, Bridgwater. His wife, Bessie Lovell Gray (also aged 40), was born in Tiverton.

15   Mrs Merson – Sarah Ann Merson (aged 44 at time of diary) married to farmer, Francis James Merson. Son, Tom Hewitt (13 at time of diary). Lived at Boomer Farm, Farringdon area of North Petherton. Flo's paternal grandmother was Mary Merson.

16   Mrs Sharp – possibly Louisa Sharp (aged 25 at time of diary) of 48 Grays Rd, Taunton. Born Exeter. Husband, Francis, was a journeyman tailor.

17   Aunt Rachael – probably Rachael Chave (aged 68 at time of diary) living at Chevithorne with her nephew in 1901. Farmed at Halberton, east of Tiverton, in 1881.

18   Blanche Hitchins – married John Cridge Brimacombe in the winter of 1897.

Friday 27th August

Wet some of day. Mother, Aunt and Blanche went for a walk, the latter hired a cycle. Rose and I cycled over to Tiverton in the afternoon for little Annie[19] had such a bad cold, didn't seem at all well.

Saturday 28th August

Mother had a cycle lesson in the morning . Father and Willie drove to Tiverton. Mother, Aunt and I went for a walk. Afterwards Mother and I strolled a little further but got caught in such a heavy shower of rain we were obliged to change. Father was out in it too but fortunately did not get wet. Rained all the afternoon. Annie no better.

Sunday 29th August

Wet. Did not go to Church. Willie[20] went to Reading. Rose and Blanche to church in the afternoon. Annie no better but rather worse.

Monday 30th August

Annie covered with a rash so Blanche and I cycled into Bampton for the doctor. He said scarlet fever and everyone must clear out that day or stay for six weeks so Mother and I drove Katie to the station and packed her off. Carrie Langdon came over in the morning. She had to go and Blanche Hitchins went in the evening. Miss King was put in head nurse.

Tuesday 31st August

Father and Mother went off. A pouring wet day. So things seemed rather dismal when we were left all alone in our glory.

---

19   Annie Persey
20   Willie – William Bond, aged 33 at time of diary, Flo's cousin and sister of Rose.

September 1897

Wednesday 1st September

Willie arrived in the morning. Another wet day so we were unable to go out. Amused ourselves by playing chess.

Thursday 2nd September

Wet again. Cleared up a bit in the afternoon. Played chess and then went mushrooming but rain came on again and we had to change our clothes. Wished we had stayed at home. Letter from Henry[1] signifying his arrival that evening.

Friday 3rd September

Henry and I took Aunt for a walk in the morning. Afternoon croquet and then Rose and I cycled to Tiverton. The air so nice and cool, it was delicious. Willie cycled to Exeter and in returning had a collision so had to leave his cycle at a cottage and return by train.

Sat 4th September

Stormy. Rose had a ride but I stayed home writing and cleaning my cycle.

Sunday 5th September

Wet again so did not go out all day. Read "A Gentleman of France."

---

1   Henry – Henry Bond, William Bond's brother and Flo's first cousin (26 yrs).

Monday 6th September

Henry took Aunt a drive in the morning and Rose and I had a cycle ride in the afternoon.

Tuesday 7th September

Henry, Rose and I took a long cycle ride to the Ruffwell. Met a funeral looking cortege, some lady who had met with an accident cycling down 'Jenny's Portion'.

Wednesday 8th September

A very wet day so we had to content ourselves indoors. Willie came back in the evening.

Thursday 9th September

Went for a walk in the morning with Aunt and Henry and persuaded Henry and Rose to cycle by themselves in the afternoon as I wanted to write.

Friday 10th September

Henry and Willie cycled to Exeter. Rose and I to Bampton and out in the morning blackberrying with Aunt Anna.[2]

Saturday 11th September

Rose and I cycled to Tiverton. No adventures till we were nearly home when Rose rode over a duck.

Sunday 12th September

A lovely day but we did not go out. Henry drove Willie to the station and brought back his friend Anstey to tea.

Monday 13th September

Rose and I rode to Tiverton. It looked so like rain that we hurried home.

---

2   Aunt Anna, one of Mrs Chave's four sisters, mother of Willie, Edward, Henry and Rose.

Tuesday 14th September

Rose, Henry and I had a lovely ride past Dulverton. It was very pretty at Dulverton. I lost the others and got on a totally different road. After enquiring and learning no cyclists had been met along that road, I turned back and got on another where I met a small boy who greeted me with, "Hurry up, they are waiting for you", and I found them calmly sitting on a bridge.

Wednesday 15th September

Went for another long ride. They said Dulverton way so of course I went that way. Could not see anything of them but at the Carnarvon Arms I heard a voice sing out, "Hullo, where are you off to?" and there was Willie on horseback. He had seen nothing of my companion but whilst I was talking to him Rose came racing after me. They had turned off on the Minehead Road. I could not help thinking such a chase served them right.

Thursday 16th September

Henry and Willie went off for a long ride on their cycles. Henry came back much the worse for it; he had had a terrible fall and hurt his face which was much bruised and swollen. Rose and I did not go out.

Friday 17th September

Henry seemed better than one would have expected. Had most amusing letters from Aunt Sophie and Mabel about the flight of my corella.[3] Another indoor day for me.

Saturday 18th September

My breakfast was enhanced by the sweet smell of an anonymous[4] box of roses and mignonette which came by post. They were so deliciously fragrant. Henry and I took Aunt for a nice walk. It poured with rain and thundered soon after our return. The afternoon was very showery so we played croquet between the showers, and chess whilst they were on.

---

3 Flo's corella – the white Australian cockatoo called "Billie"

4 Possibly from Dr McCutchan?

Sunday 19th September

Not a bad day but we stayed in all day.

Monday 20th September

A lovely day. We rode to Winsford after dinner. Went on Exmoor and picked quite a nice lot of staghorn moss. Had a cup of tea, then rode back at such a rate as it was quite dark long before we reached home.

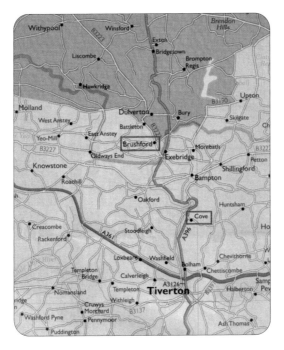

Map showing Brushford.

The Carnarvon Arms Hotel was at Brushford. Built in 1874, to serve Dulverton Station, guests included Alfred Lord Tennyson and – it is rumoured – the Beatles.

Tuesday 21st September

Stormy day. Rose and Henry were going to Torquay but too unpromising so we did not do much.

Wednesday 22nd September

Rose and Henry cycled off to Torquay early in the morning. Aunt and I went for a walk and picked a basketful of blackberries. Spent a quiet afternoon reading and working. Willie came back soon after 5 and Rose and Henry about 8.30. They had had a wretched day, so wet, and Rose had gone and returned by train.

Thursday 23rd September

Henry left us in the morning. Rose and I did not feel much inclined for exertion so had a quiet day.

Friday 24th September

Very windy so we decided to forgo cycling and took Aunt for a walk in the afternoon, not a nice day for exertion, so hot.

Saturday 25th September

Willie, Rose and I rode to Tiverton in the morning. Back to a later dinner after which we played croquet till tea time. Mr White came whilst we were at tea and spent most of the evening.

Sunday 26th September

Rose and I drove in with Willie. Rather exciting as the wheel nearly came off, only held on by one nut which Willie had to keep on jumping out to screw in. We changed traps to return home. A lovely afternoon, quite hot and summerlike.

Monday 27th September

Rose and I rode to Exeter after dinner and got back about 7.30. It was a nice ride but rather too dark coming back. We had about one hour in Exeter.

Wednesday 29th September

Very wet but I drove in town with Willie in the morning and spent most of the afternoon and evening playing chess.

Thursday 30th September

Rose and Annie went for a walk and came back wet through such a storm of rain. Too wet to do anything save chess for the rest of the day.

October 1897

Friday 1st October

Rose and I took a very short cycle ride but it was rather an exciting one as we met a lot of hunting people and had a grand view of the stag which passed along a field close to the road where we were standing. The hunted looked far nobler than the hunters.

Saturday 2nd October

Rose and I rode to Bickleigh. It got rather dark before we returned. Saw Mr & Mrs ?Carew.

Sunday 3rd October

As usual, a quiet, indoor day.

Monday 4th October

Rose went for a short ride. I did not go out.

Tuesday 5th October

Was going for a ride but my tyre was flat so we both stayed at home.

Wednesday 6th October

Was walking into Tiverton with my cycle. Overtaken by an ironmonger who picked me up and was back again before Rose started to meet me. Not a puncture but valve leakage for which I was very glad. Willie, Rose and I then cycled to Collipriest. Willie killed a snake which was crossing the road right between our cycles. It was thin but long and very brightly marked.

Thursday 7th October

Rose and I just rode to Tiverton, forgetting it was shut shop day. Annie and Miss King??.

Friday 8th October

Rode in again but it came on a nasty drizzle so we stopped no longer than we could help.

Sunday 10th October

Went to church afternoon, wet but we drove Willie to Tiverton.

Monday 11th October

Wet rather, but a nice evening. Rose and I celebrated our freedom again by driving into Tiverton and going to see the "Geisha". It was very pretty and rather amusing.

Tuesday 12th October

Got ready to go to Exeter but found Rose had a valve leakage so had it repaired Tiverton and rode to Silverton and took tea with the May's.

Wednesday 13th October

Aunt and Rose wet to meet Willie, and he and Rose cycled in the afternoon. Willie and I had the best game of chess we have had at all. It ended in a stalemate.

Friday 15th October

Another day indoors wet, so most of the afternoon and evening were devoted to chess.

Saturday 16th October

Drove to Tiverton with Willie in the morning and did a lot of shopping. It was a treat to have a nice morning again. Rose and Willie took a walk in the afternoon.

Sunday 17ᵗʰ October

Rose and I went for a long walk with Willie and went to church in the afternoon.

Cover of the vocal score of Sidney Jones' musical comedy, *The Geisha*.
[Wikipedia]

Bickleigh Mill Stream and Bridge
Photo: Lewis Clarke [Wikipedia]

Monday 18th October

Went a cycle ride to Tiverton. Rose punctured her tyre so we had to walk back from the ?Fish

Tuesday 19th October

Was rather dull and rainy. Rose and Aunt walked to Bampton in the afternoon. There was such a lovely sunset.

Wednesday 20th October

Rose and I rode to Tiverton. The roads were frightful. We took train to Exeter. Enjoyed ourselves there shopping about two hours and then rode home. The roads as far as "Jennie's Portion" atrocious. After that they were better and we got home in very good time.

Thursday 21st October

Rose drove us to town and we went to see Crocker's Educated Horses. They were splendid – waltzed, seesawed, bowed, fetched and carried all to command. The scene "Field by Jury" was very good. We walked nearly all the way home as we left the trap for Willie.

Friday 22nd October

Rose drove me in to catch the 2.50 train and I went to Torquay. Arrived there about tea time. Did not surprise them very much. Went out in the evening to make an appointment with the dentist, then Eliza Chave at Bean ?Cove

Saturday 23rd October

Went to the dentist in the morning. Also inspected the shops. Aunt Elise and Eliza went out to Miss Mogridge's. Were not home till after 8. Aunt's next door neighbour has come as boarder for a short time. He is a funny old man of 81, puffs and blows so and talks to himself. He was ? distressing and seems quite childish.

Sunday 24th October

Went to All Saints by myself. The old gent seems a little revived. Anna stayed home with him. In the evening Aunt Sophie and I went to St Luke's.

Monday 25th October

Went to the dentist in the afternoon. Eliza rushed in before we were up in the morning to tell us the poor old fellow was groaning and grunting to himself and saying, "O Mrs Lang, Mrs Lang, what have you done, what have you done, what a shame, what a shame!" In the evening we went to a lecture on "The Marvellous Boy" (Thomas Chatterton) given by Rev Dawson. I did not altogether like him.

Tuesday 26th October

Started for Cove about 11 and had a very quiet journey. Rose and Little Annie met me at the station and drove me home.

Wednesday 27th October

Willie and Mr Stone arrived to dinner. Annie and Miss King walked to Tiverton and Aunt and I went part way with them. Mr Lavor came to tea and Mr Harris and grandson to supper, all staying the night.

Thursday 28th October

All the gents gone by the time I arrived down. Bampton Fair Day. The roads were quite gay with traffic. Our letters all contained bad news. Nellie Lang[1] is ill. They had to have three doctors in consultation. Miss King walked into Tiverton to see the Carnival.

Friday 29th October

Better news of Cousin Nellie. Rose drove Annie and I to Tiverton. Met Miss King returning but without Rose's cycle which she took in Wed and is not done yet.

---

[1]   Nellie Lang – Helen Lang, daughter of Mrs Chave's sister, Sophia. Aged 39 at time of diary. She and her sisters ran Culcheth Hall School in Bowdon, Cheshire, where Flo's youngest sister, Ivy, attended in 1891. Possibly this is also where her sister Mabel was a governess. Helen died in 1898.

Professor Crocker's Educated Horses 1899 – Library of Congress [Wikipedia]

Born in Hillsdale County in Michigan, Professor Crocker travelled Europe, performing with his "educated horses, ponies, donkeys and mules" for twenty years.

"The Death of Chatterton" by Henry Wallis, 1856 [Wikipedia]

Thomas Chatterton (1752–70) was an English poet who passed off his work as that of Thomas Rowley, an imaginary 15th century poet. Chatterton committed suicide aged 17.

Saturday 30th October

Willie, Rose (her cycle arrived night before) and I went for a short cycle ride. It was quite a treat again and the roads were lovely.

Sunday 31st October

Went to church with Miss King. Rose and I drove into town in the afternoon with Willie, put up our horse and took tea with Miss Ellerton.[2] Went to St Peter's in the evening. It was very dark returning.

---

2   Miss Ellerton – probably Muriel Bessie Ellerton of Fore Street, Tiverton, aged 20 at time of diary. Her father, John Francis Ellerton, was one time Mayor of Tiverton.

November 1897

Monday 1st November

Rose and I rode into Tiverton in the morning and came back to late dinner, after which Rose rode into Bampton but I had had enough. There was too much wind to suit me so I stayed at home.

Tuesday 2nd November

We rushed into Tiverton, returning a different way to Bolham to get a cake for Eva Goddard's[1] tea and after all she did not come.

Wednesday 3rd November

We rode over to see Aunt Rachael. Eliza's machine is bought but she had not got it. We had an early tea and rode home in 1 hr and a quarter. It would have been a lovely trip but the wind was so high, quite gale like at times. Willie was expected but did not return.

Thursday 4th November

Rode into Tiverton in the morning. Very cold. Rose went out again in the afternoon, but I didn't. Willie arrived home about tea and found a small party here consisting of Eva Goddard and her brother, George.

Friday 5th November

Rode into Tiverton in morning and back to dinner. Willie started on his cycle en route for Dunster. On his way punctured his tyre so had to wire for the horse and trap to be sent after him.

---

1   Eva Goddard – 24 at time of diary. Lived at Burn Hayes, next door to the Bond cousins in Bickleigh in 1891. Eva was a school governess.

Saturday 6th November

Mrs and Miss Ellerton[2] came to tea so we did not go out all day. Willie and Rose had to escort them to the station.

Sunday 7th November

Rose and I stayed Communion. In the morning drove Willie to Tiverton. In the afternoon Miss King went to Bampton in the evening and had to come home in the wet.

Monday 8th November

Did not go out all day as too damp for cycling. Rose painted and I chipped.

Tuesday 9th November

Not promising looking. We were to have cycled out to dinner with the Tapps but the roads looked too unpropitious so we painted instead.

Wednesday 10th November

A nice day. We should have gone to Miss Tapp's but just before going to get ready, Rose discovered screw loose in her machine so she and Willie rode into Tiverton and I chipped. They said the roads were atrocious so it was lucky we could not go.

Thursday 11th November

Wet again so did not go out but did some painting and chipping. Great excitement in the morning as the poor old Persia cat was caught in a gin on the lawn. Poor thing was soon released and did not seem much hurt.

Gin traps were banned in Britain in 1954. Flo's younger brother, Harold, wrote to a newspaper in 1889 about their cat being caught in a gin trap:

> *Dear Uncle Oldman,*
>
> *I want very much to become a member of the Guild of Kindness. Will you tell me all about it, please, dear Uncle Oldman? Some years ago a*

---

2   Mrs and Miss Ellerton – probably Florence (aged 38) Ellerton (wife of grocer, John Ellerton of 7–9 Fore Street, Tiverton) and her daughter, Muriel (aged 20).

cat strayed from the next farmhouse to ours, and, as they did not want him, we kept him. We called him Tom. He was very funny. He would get between our feet, and try to throw us down. One night, as the man who works for us went up into the loft to get some hay, he saw the cat there. He was quite startled, and he called for another of our men. He came, and they found the cat had his leg in a trap. They instantly loosed the poor cat, and found that his claws were cut right off one leg. Where he got caught in the trap we do not know, nor how he dragged the trap up into the loft, about 20ft. high; and you may imagine the pain it caused him; but he walks along quite happily on his three legs.

HAROLD L CHAVE (age 10).

The Moor House, Hereford.

[The Manchester Times, 1889]

Friday 12th November

Wet and dull again so we did not go out but played chess (one game only) in the morning, and chipped all afternoon. This weather is lovely for one's work.

Saturday 13th November

Pouring wet morning but cleared in the afternoon so I drove into Tiverton with Willie. 1st time I had been out since Sunday so it was quite a treat.

Sunday 14th November

Rose and I went to church in the morning. Stayed home rest of day. Miss King went to Bampton and took tea with the Goddards and had her usual wet return.

Monday 15th November

Rose and I drove into town. After dinner called on Mrs Rawlings[3] but she was not at home. We were not very grieved. Then on Mrs Anstey – reached home at 6, very cold.

---

3   Mrs Rawlings, vicar's wife. Arthur Rawlings was vicar of Cove in 1891. By 1901 had moved to Tiverton.

Tuesday 16th November

Rose and I drove to Tiverton, took the 11 train to Stoke. Met Aunts there. Aunt Sophie and I had lunch with the Robsons[4] and Aunt Elise and Rose called to enquire for Mrs Trenton, poor soul is in such awful pain. They cannot wish her to live. All met at the station and took train to Exeter where we stayed rest of the day. Took tea with Miss Luget. It was not a nice day – a drizzle all the time. Such a dark night. We were glad when Cove was reached.

Wednesday 17th November

Willie's birthday. He returned about 5 o'clock. Rose and I did not go out all day. Aunt Anna had a rubber with us in the evening. A wire from Edward.[5] He had arrived in London but could not get through that evening.

Thursday 18th November

Willie and I had a game of chess in the morning. Again I was twice defeated. Edward arrived about 6 looking very well and just himself. He seems to have had a good time.

Friday 19th November

Willie cycled to Tiverton and Rose drove Ed. I stayed home and had it all to myself as Aunt and Miss King went for a walk. Rose and Willie cycled in the afternoon and I drove with Edward to Morebath Station to get his luggage.

Saturday 20th November

Rose and Willie again cycled. I stayed home (roads too muddy) and Edward and I amused ourselves with chess.

Sunday 21st November

Church with Rose in the morning. Inclined to be wet so stayed at home rest of the day. Willie went off as usual and Edward escorted him to the station.

---

4   The Robsons, Rev Frederick Robson (54 yrs) and his wife, Elizabeth (34 yrs), lived at the Vicarage, Stoke Canon in 1901.

5   Edward Bond, Flo's first cousin, brother of Rose, Willie and Henry. (28 yrs). Lived at Cove Place House 1901. Cider merchant.

Monday 22nd November

Eva Goddard and Lucy Batten paid Rose a morning call and stayed to dinner.

Tuesday 23rd November

Edward spent the day in Tiverton, and Rose and I spent it in the house.

Wednesday 24th November

Willie returned. Aunt and Miss King went for a walk. Edward fetched Willie and Rose and the latter cycled in the afternoon but it was not tempting enough for me.

Thursday 25th November

Edward drove me to Widhayes[6] to dinner. We spent a pleasant three hours there and returned in time for tea. Very cold driving.

Friday 26th November

Willie and I played chess all the afternoon, and Edward and Rose drove to Tiverton.

Saturday 27th November

Spent the morning finishing the owls I commenced last night. Wet morning to begin with.

Sunday 28th November

Very wet morning so did not go to church. Afternoon, if anything, was worse. Willie did not go to Reading.

29th November, 30th November, 1st December – Mon, Tues and Wed. all much the same. Rain rain rain. Edward and I went for a walk the last morning. He seemed so depressed, it seemed to cheer him up a bit but the weather was terrible.

---

6   Widhayes Farm, Uplowman, was where Edward Chave (45 yrs) and his family lived. Edward was the son of Mr Chave's brother, Edward Chave. His son, John Haydon Chave, was killed in France in 1918.

December 1897

Thursday 2nd December

Willie went away very early, not coming back till tomorrow evening. Miss King also going away to stay till Monday. The weather very windy but nice and brighter, quite refreshing.

Friday 3rd December

Spent the afternoon packing. Rose took a cycle ride and in evening I nearly finished my book "Evan Harrington" which I like very much.

Saturday 4th December

Rode my cycle to Tiverton 1st time for a month. Rose came in lunch time. Edward came by train from Bampton. I joined him and we proceeded to Torquay, Rose accompanying us as far as Bickleigh.

Sunday 5th December

Went to church with Edward, and Aunt Sophie to Ellacombe in the morning to hear Aunt's pet, Canon Atherson, and again in the evening Aunt Elise and I went to fetch Aunt Sophie who had taken tea with the ?Lanards.

Monday 6th December

Took Edward for a walk in the morning. Miss Tavener and Mrs Robson came to tea. Evening we went to hear Rev Clarke "on Dickens". He was as usual very good.

Illustration for Chapter 10 of George Meredith's 'Evan Harrington'
"While waking to Fallowfield at night, Evan finds a woman huddled miserably on a stone and offers her aid."
Engraving by Joseph Swain 1860. [Wikipedia]

Malvern, the Promenade Gardens – Francis Bedford 1816–94 –
National Media Museum [Wikipedia]

Tuesday 7th December

Went to Miss Mogridge's to dinner and tea. A most atrocious day as far as the weather was concerned. We had to get a cab from the village to take us back to the station.

Wednesday 8th December

Edward left us. We did not go out all day until the evening when Aunts went to church.

Thursday 9th December

Went to a bazaar in the morning but did not buy anything. Anna went out to tea and Aunts to a nursing lecture so Mr Pope and I were left all alone.

Friday 10th December

Pouring wet morning but cleared up in the afternoon. Mrs Pope intended leaving but was afraid to venture. Mrs Sharp, Mrs Dallday (her sister and the latter's little boy) arrived.

Saturday 11th December

Aunt Elise left for Rose's in the morning. Mr Pope also left. Anna went to a concert, the Sharps to Paignton and Aunt Sophie and I went to town and do the shops.

Sunday 12th December

Such a wet morning. Aunt Sophie alone was brave enough to venture to church. The afternoon cleared up and Aunt and I went to Trinity in the evening.

Monday 13th December

The Sharps left after dinner, so Anna, Aunt and I are all alone. A wet day again. Aunt Sophie went round Aunt Elise's district but I did not venture out.

Tuesday 14th December

Aunt went to town and Anna and I went but we did not encounter each other. Anna and I went to a sale but were not charmed with the house and saw nothing we wanted to buy. The garden was pretty being a terraced one with lovely view over the sea to Paignton. Miss Mogridge came to spend the afternoon and it turned out so wet and miserable she was obliged to stay the night.

Wednesday 15th December

We again inspected shops in the morning. Edith Persey and another young lady (Miss Hopkins) came to tea and supper. The evening wet as usual.

Thursday 16th December

Not a tempting morning. Still we sallied forth after an early dinner and found it not so bad. The evening I spent by myself as Aunt and Anna went to their nursing lecture.

Friday 17th December

Aunt Sophie and I went to town in the morning and this time successful in buying Mother and Anna their presents. Miss Lees came to dinner, also Capt. Hall, Miss Pollie Mogridge just popped in for a few seconds to fetch her uncle in the afternoon. Anna went to her drill in the evening.

Saturday 18th December

Very busy day packing; Walked in town in the morning and did not go out rest of day though it was beautifully spring like. Ethel Mogridge spent the day.

Sunday 19th December

Went to Upton in the morning and to Trinity in the evening. Edith Persey spent the day with us.

December 1897 continued

Flo and her family move to a hotel in Malvern. At this time, The Moor House was let. Members of the family staying the night in Hereford, would stay in Hewitt's house, adjacent to the Moor House and the cider works, when in Hereford.

Monday 20th December

We started off, our baggage and ourselves in due time, and met Aunt Elise at Taunton. It was a tiresome journey. We had to change 4 times and it was very cold and bleak. Mother and Hewitt[1] met us at the station. "Billie" behaved well. Father was looking much better and the hotel seems very nice and comfortable. Poor old Hewitt is rather upset by his old lady who seems to be going out of her mind. Aunt and Nellie[2] had arrived about 3.

Tuesday 21st December

Father went to Hereford to see how the poor old soul is. She is not allowed to be left though she seems perfectly quiet. Mother, Aunt and I spent the day inspecting the shops. Cousin Nellie looks very ill and feels very tired after her journey. I just had a glimpse of her. She was down yesterday but seems much better and brighter today.

Wednesday 22nd December

Father received a frightful anonymous letter from London threatening to put a bullet through him. Some of the language was far too choice to be repeated. It also said he should be on the look out for the cyclists (that's Mabel and me), poor old Hewitt and the grey woman (Mother) and ended up with "and now take the curse of Dick Mallard" or some such name.

Father went to Hereford. They have decided to send the poor old lady to William's for a few weeks and Hewitt will come over here. Aunt Elise and I rode to Worcester, a long ride but so muddy. Got back in time for lunch and did not go out again.

---

1   Hewitt – Edward W Hewitt Chave Flo's younger brother (aged 24 at time of diary). Ran cider business for father. Married first cousin Rose Bond in 1908. The "old lady" was possibly his housekeeper.

2   Nellie – presumably Nellie Lang.

Father laughs at his letter but it makes me feel very uneasy, especially after poor Mr Terriss' assassination and the writer does not seem a bit more mad than that man. They think it comes from a Miss Hill who was boarding here and left last Saturday because she fell out with Mrs Hollingsworth and Mother.

Thursday 23rd December

Father and I walked down and saw Mother off to Hereford. In the afternoon Father and I again went to the station to meet Mabel. Mother and Hewitt came in the evening. The poor old cook has gone to William's quite peacefully and Hewitt has closed his establishment.

Friday 24th December

Shopping nearly all day. Mabel and Aunt Elise had a cycle ride but I was too busy.

Saturday 25th December 1897 – Xmas Day

The presents were all a success apparently. It was a lovely day, quite an ideal Xmas. Father and I took a walk in the morning. Everything was looking so bright and nice. We enjoyed it. We went to a short afternoon service at the Abbey at 4.30 p.m.

A cycling purse – Aunt Sophie

Pair of bedroom slippers – Aunt Elise

30/- from Father

Paper knife from Ivy

A purse from Mabel

And many Xmas cards but the letter that was sent to me was addressed Dear Berifice and was evidently meant for someone else.

Jessie Millward and William Terriss in The Harbour Lights circa 1890 –
Jessie Millward Myself and Others [Wikipedia]

William Terriss was one of Britain's most popular swashbuckling actors of the
time. He played the hero parts in melodramas at the Adelphi Theatre in London
from the late 1880s, and in 1897 he was stabbed to death by a fellow actor,
Richard Archer Prince, at the stage door. His ghost is said to haunt Covent
Garden tube station and the Adelphi Theatre.

Broad Street and Free Library, Hereford circa 1880 [Wikipedia]

Sunday 26ᵗʰ December

Went to the Abbey and took Aunt Sophie Lang[3] in the morning. Aunt Elise and I had tea with the invalid, went to the Abbey again in the evening.

Monday 27ᵗʰ December

Aunt Sophie had a letter saying poor Willie Langdon[4] has died Christmas Eve. He has been ill a long time. It was not a nice day. I spent most of it mending clothes. The others took a little fresh air.

Tuesday 28ᵗʰ December

It looked a nice morning but came on to rain. Cleared up again in the afternoon. Two fresh people, a doctor and his wife, came in. I did not go out all day. Mother and Mabel walked to the top of the hill. Mr Jackson[5] came for about two hours on his way back from Birmingham.

Wednesday 29ᵗʰ December

Mother and Aunt Elise started by the 11 train to Bristol. Poor Willie is to be buried today, a very wet day. Aunt and Mother returned about 8.30.

Thursday 30ᵗʰ December

Cousin Nellie went out. Father, Mabel and I took a walk round the "Ladies Walk". The wind very cold. Mother, Mrs MacDonald and Aunts took a stroll. Aunt Sophie Lang and Mrs Hollingsworth were the stylish ones and took a drive.

Friday 31ˢᵗ December

Mother, Aunts, Mabel and Mrs MacDonald climbed the hill in the morning. May and I went shopping in the afternoon. There was a great row in the house in the morning, the cook having had to be sent off at a moment's notice for drunkenness. She was such a good cook, too.

---

3   Aunt Sophie Lang (69 yrs) – Mrs Chave's aunt and mother of Cousin Nellie. She died in Bowden, Lancs in 1900.

4   Willie Langdon (36 yrs) – son of Mrs Chave's eldest sister, Sarah, and brother to Anna and Carrie.

5   Mr Jackson – probably the Mr Jackson who bought Mr Chave's chemist shop from him in 1879. Living with wife, Annie at 6–7 Broad Street in 1891.

Mabel's bookmark [By kind permission of HARC]

Flo's draft monograms [By kind permission of HARC]

January 1898

Saturday 1st January

Not at all a promising day. Such a fog all day. Most of them ventured out once except me and I spent the day indoors. Expected Dr Mac but he never came. Rather afraid my letter must have offended.

Sunday 2nd January

I did not go to church in the morning. No letter. Hope it's not serious. Went to the Abbey in the evening.

Monday 3rd January

Started off first thing after breakfast to Cox and Painter sale. Bought a jacket. Left by 2.47 train for Hereford. Fell in with the Clarksons[1] at station just when I did not wish to meet with any of my friends as I was acting the part of knight errant to my travelling companion who seemed much bothered with two children and a parcel. At Mrs Lloyd's[2] I must needs to venture too near her gas stove and singe a great hole in my dress. The children's party in the evening was a great success, Mr Jacob,[3] Miss Britten[4] and I were the

---

1   Edith Clarkson (26 yrs) daughter of Henry Clarkson, grocer and wine merchant, living at Bodenham Rd Crescent, Tupsley, Hereford in 1891.

2   Mrs Lloyd – Mrs Emily Edith Lloyd (aged 38 yrs) wife of William G Lloyd, JP (said to be a descendant of the poet, Milton), and mother of Robert Stuart Lloyd (11 yrs) and William Frank Lloyd (13 yrs). Lived at Oaklands, Bodenham Rd, Tupsley, Hereford in 1901.

3   Mr Jacob – probably Mr John Hier Jacob (36 at time of diary) Solicitor, of Cradock House, Tupsley. He was given the OBE in 1918.

4   Edith Britten – there was a 13 year old Edith Britten at Hereford High School in 1891.

only grown ups. My expected letter arrived by mid day post. It ought to have reached me in the morning but had gone to Worcester. Dr M could not come Saturday though he had intended doing so.

Dr William Arthur McCutchan at The Gables, Stoke sub Hamdon, Somerset – between 1890 and 1894

Photo: Dr W A McCutchan

Invitation from the Clarksons
[By kind permission of HARC]

Tuesday 4th January

Mrs Lloyd walked in town with me in the afternoon, then I went and called on the Clarksons and had afternoon tea. Then went to Etta's[5] and had tea. Left about 8 and took a cab back. Found Min Terrabee there. Mr & Mrs Moore returned from Malvern whilst I was there so were able to give me all the latest news.

Wednesday 5th January

Aunt Sophie Lang, Nellie, Aunt Elise and the nurse left Malvern for Sidmouth. I met them at Hereford Station and spent half an hour with them. Their invalid carriage made them look quite swell. Then I went to Hewitt's and back to Mrs Lloyd's to tea. Mrs Jones and Mrs Jacob were there for the evening. Frank and Stuart had gone to Thowle for a week.

Thursday 6th January

Mr Jacob left early. Mrs Lloyd, Miss Terrabee and I walked into town and after dinner Mrs Lloyd and I saw Miss Terrabee off then we returned home and were too comfortable to turn out for the photographic display.

Friday 7th January

Stayed home all the morning. Paid calls in the afternoon. Mrs Wylie 1st place. We met just outside her gate. Mrs Riley we found at home, also Mrs Cooke and Miss Friend. We partook of afternoon tea both places and did not go out again though there was an organ recital on.

Sat 8th.

Mother came by 11 train. I met her and we went to Hewitt's, took provisions and had a nice little picnic luncheon to ourselves there. Returned to Malvern by 4 train. Edward Bond arrived yesterday.

Sunday 9th January

Father's birthday. I had such a bad cold, did not go out all day.

---

5   Henrietta Baker (27 yrs) stepdaughter of Dr Henry Moore (Medical Officer of Health, born Lucknow, India) 26 Broad Street, Hereford.

Monday 10th January

Aunt, Mabel, Mother and Edward took a very long walk to British Camp and took their lunch with them. Father and I took the afternoon bus to W Malvern and walked home. Lost the dog on the way. He turned up alright but dead tired. Found poor "Little Billie" in sad disgrace – made such a noise, they banished him from the drawing room and he has to return to the smoke room.

Malvern Hills from British Camp
Photo: Gail Hampshire [Wikipedia]

282. Malvern—St. Ann's Well.

St. Ann's Well, Great Malvern 1860s by Francis Bedford [Wikipedia]

Tuesday 11th January

Hewitt and his dog left in the morning. Selina Johnson, his new housekeeper comes tomorrow. Mother, Mabel, Edward, Aunt and I took a lovely long walk over the M. Hills. The day was rather dark looking and a north east wind but we enjoyed it. Got home to lunch, and afternoon Mother and I spent at Cox and Painter's. Back to afternoon tea. Mother, Edward and Aunt called on Mrs Chappel.

Wednesday 12th January

Mother and Aunt went to Hereford, were pleased with the new housekeeper's appearance. Father, Mabel and Edward took a walk in the morning. I was busy indoors. In the afternoon, Edward and I walked round the hills, through the Wych and back W. & N. Malvern, passed the stocks on our way. I had never seen any before.

Thursday 13th January

Mother, Aunt Sophie and Edward spent the day with Mrs Brimmacombe *[Blanche Hitchins]*. They discovered her through Hewitt's housekeeper advertisement. One of the applicants gave a reference to Mrs Chapple who lives here and is a Tiverton lady, so when they were calling to enquire about her, of course Mrs C. was delighted to see them and had other callers who turned out to be Blanche and her sister and so she fixed the day for them to come and dine with her. May and I were left alone as Father went to Hereford. We did not go out. It was foggy and untempting.

Friday 14th January

Aunt Sophie left by the morning train. Father, Mother and I went down to see her off and then waited for Mac's train but he did not appear so I went down to meet the next, then I took him for a walk to St Anne's Well and round the Ladies' Walk, returning in time for afternoon tea. Edward and Mabel had been away ever since breakfast, walking all along the ranges. They returned about an hour before Mac left so were able to make his acquaintance and to my relief formed an impression that was favourable rather than otherwise. Then I took him the short cut to the station. He told me of Dr Morrison's[6] engagement. The lady was a surprise to me. I rode back in the bus but wished I had walked for I would have been back before it started.

Flo's father,
Mr William Francis Chave at
The Moor House, Hereford ca 1895
Photo: Dr W A McCutchan

Flo Chave at The Moor House,
Hereford ca 1895
Photo: Dr W A McCutchan

6   Dr Cuthbert Stanislaus Morrison, born Bengal, India (36 years at time of diary). Medical Superintendent of Burghill Mental Asylum., Cheshire. Mac spent 6 months working with Dr Morrison as a medical student when he was in private practice in Wrenbury. Dr Morrison married Margaret Wheatley who was 11 years younger than himself.

Saturday 15th January

Edward and I had early breakfast. Mrs MacDonald had it with us as she was leaving for London so our numbers now are greatly reduced. We got to Birmingham about ten, found it very cold and were not greatly impressed with the town. We walked over a good portion of it, saw the Museum and Art Gallery which was interesting.

Could not find our way into the Town Hall, had lunch at the London Restaurant and then walked out to see Aston Park. There was a grand football match in the Lower Grounds and it was a sight to see the people streaming to it. The trains were full and a regular stream of cabs going and returning, 40,000 people. Thousands had to be refused admission.

Aston Park grounds were nothing much to our mind but we went into the Old Hall and inspected it and were very pleased. Saw a writing cabinet with 4 drawers in it that had belonged to Charles I, and the centre was a mirror so that when he was writing he could see behind him. It was in a very fine old gallery. There was also a clock still going that belonged to Shakespeare. The Hall contained 107 rooms. It was besieged and taken by Cromwell and the hole made in the staircase with a cannon ball is still shewn.

There is a collection of birds, shells and a few curios to be seen, a small room the entrance of which forms a chair so was probably a secret chamber.

The 1st founder imprisoned his daughter in a wretched little garret with hardly any light in it because she eloped with a groom in preference to marrying someone he wished her to. She was liberated when Cromwell took the place but was then insane. We got back in very good time for dinner. I enjoyed the day very much.

Sunday 16th January

Went to church in the morning but so foggy and nasty we did not venture out again. Hewitt came over to lunch. Poor old fellow has a wretched cold.

Monday 17th January

Such a nasty fog. We did not go out except to do a little shopping in the morning. Spent the afternoon sewing. Ethel Ballard[7] called and had

---

7   Ethel Ballard – married Stephen Ballard, Vinegar Manufacturer (a cousin perhaps) in 1894. She lived in Holmer, Hereford prior to her marriage, and in 1901 lived in Colwall, not far from Great Malvern.

afternoon tea with us. 1st time I have seen her since her marriage. I have been meaning to call if only the weather would cheer up a bit so shall now go 1st fine day.

Tuesday 18th January

Mabel left in the morning. We all went to see her off. Then Edward, Mother and I walked to the Link. It was not very tempting so Father did not accompany us but returned to the hotel.

Wednesday 19th January

Father and Edward went to Hereford. Mother and I saw them off. It was a very nasty morning so we went no further but spent the rest of the day at home. Father came back. Edward is spending rest of his visit with Hewitt.

Thursday 20th January

Mother and I went into the town and made a few purchases, then Father and Mother went a short stroll, the former not at all himself. The afternoon was much nicer so I went over to see Ethel by the 3 train meaning to return by the 4.30 but the time slipped away so quickly and pleasantly that the train had gone before I even thought of leaving.

Friday 21st January

Father still very bad. Did not get up till after his breakfast and did not go out all day. The afternoon was lovely. Mother and I walked to the Wells to see the "Holy Well" and found a beautiful way house across the hills which brought us out below the "Wych" cutting. It was a beautiful walk and we got grand views. New boarder arrived Wednesday. She is called Leigh and seems intimately acquainted with all the aristocracy and is a great talker.

Saturday 22nd January

Father did not get up to breakfast. Still he seems a trifle better, but did not venture out. Mother and I did a five mile walk to see Newlands Church, a modern one, very small but beautifully decorated with frescoes etc.

Sunday 23rd January

Mother and I went to Emmanuel Church in the morning. Very nice service. It is the Countess of Huntington. Found Edward and Hewitt had arrived on our return and heard Mr Jackson was on the way. He turned up not long after. Took the boys for a walk in the afternoon and met with Mr & Mrs Alfred Watkins[8] who with their children are staying at the "Wych". Mother and I went to the same church again in the evening.

Monday 24th January

Father and Mother sallied out in quest of a brine bath but found there were none to be had till the season begins. Mrs Watkins called in the afternoon and Mother and I walked back to the "Wych" with her.

Tuesday 25th January

Left by the 11.7 train so had to do my packing in an awful hurry as I had not intended leaving till after lunch but Father's society tempted me. He returned again by the 4 train. Hewitt and I walked to station and saw him off, returning round town met Mrs Lloyd and soon after Mrs Jackson.[9]

Wednesday 26th January

Read and worked all the morning. Hewitt left for Devon about 12. Walked in town in the afternoon. Met Mrs Jackson who invited me to a concert Friday evening but I declined. Called on the Ballards. They were not at home. Invited Miss Woodyate to tea tomorrow.

Thursday 27th January

Father arrived about 12. We had a nice little dinner together. He left by 4 train. I walked to station with him, returned through town, found Miss W. had arrived. She stayed till the last bus. Had a quiet time but I think she enjoyed it.

---

8   Mr & Mrs Alfred Watkins – Mr Chave and Alfred Watkins were joint Vice Presidents of Hereford's Chamber of Commerce. This was very probably the Alfred Watkins of photography and ley line fame.

9   Mrs Jackson – Annie Jackson, wife of J J Jackson of Jackson & Chave, 6-7 Broad Street, Hereford

Friday 28th January

Mother came soon after 11, then we went to town and reached Mrs Moore's about 1. Etta looking so much better. We had dinner and afternoon tea and spent very pleasant afternoon. Mrs Ed. Moore and her daughter from Birmingham were there. Mother left by 6.15 train. I walked down and saw her off. Reached home about 7 and spent a quiet evening reading.

Saturday 29th January

Started for Malvern by 9.40 train. Found Father and Mother awaiting me. The day turned out nice and bright but very cold wind. We went a short walk and then returned to lunch. Miss Leigh had gone to Worcester. Otherwise all seemed much the same.

After dinner Mother and I spent the afternoon shopping, then I rode down to the station on my cycle. Mother luckily walked down to see me off otherwise I found I hadn't enough money to pay my fare so it would have been rather awkward for me. Rode my cycle back from station. Quite a treat to mount it again.

Found a note awaiting me from Mac saying he would be in in the evening so I had a pleasant time. He was very good and left early. There are some theatricals next Thursday at the C.C.A. I should like to go but am afraid I shall not be able to arrange it.

Mother had a lady to call on her in the morning. She called yesterday but finding no one at home, left her name, "Miss Davies" and said she would call next day at the same hour. We cannot think which Miss Davies it was and never thought of the right one. It was May Davies and she is "boarding" in Malvern by herself for a short time as she has not been very well.

Sunday 30th January

Went to the Cathedral in the morning and did not go out rest of day but wrote and read. Mrs Johnson went for a walk in the afternoon.

Monday 31st January

Rode into town to get some fish for dinner. Father was so late I had just come to the conclusion he had lost his train when he turned up. Mrs Jackson called on her cycle and wanted me to go for a ride but I could not go before

4 and she could not go after which was rather lucky as Mrs Lloyd came whilst Father and I were having tea. She had left word Sat. she would come but Mrs Johnson told me Thursday so of course I was not at all expecting her. We rode to Mansell Lacey and back. The roads were lovely – found Mrs Evans had called whilst I was out.

The Sign of the Cross was an 1895 play by Wilson Barrett. It was the basis for a 1932 film adaptation directed by Cecil B DeMille. Barrett's daughter, Dorothea protested against it be made into a film, "I loathe and abominate the films."
[Wikipedia]

Park Lane with Omnibus – Watercolour by Rose Maynard Barton (1856–1929)
[Wikipedia]

February 1898

Tuesday 1st February

Had a busy morning cleaning my machine which badly needed it. After dinner, walked to town and changed my book, "Sign of the Cross" with which I was rather disappointed for "Stories of Naples – the Camorra" by Chas. Grant. Called on Etta and invited her to drive with me tomorrow. Mrs Lloyd came to tea just before 6 and left 7.30. We talk of riding to Malvern Friday next.

Wednesday 2nd February

Had a nice note and lots of papers from Mac, brought by one of the attendants. Rode in in the bus and called for Etta and brought her back in the fly. Father never came till 1.32 train and had had his lunch which was rather annoying as I had quite a nice little spread for him. Took Etta back in a cab and walked home. Father left 6.15 so I went down to the station and saw him off and walked home. It was not at all nice, such a high wind and so keen. It has been trying to hail and snow all day.

Thursday 3rd February

A high wind and towards evening wet so did not go out except just over the bridge after tea to post a letter. A visitor in the afternoon on his cycle, Stuart Lloyd, to say his mother could not ride with me to Malvern next day.

Friday 4th February

Turned out very wet so we could not have gone in any case. I did not go outside the door but read and worked all day.

Saturday 5th February

Rode my cycle over to Huntington. Found a very sick household as Mrs Lock has influenza. Clem Murch[1] a bad leg and poor Tom[2] looked dreadful. He is evidently in the last stage of consumption and has to be carried up and down stairs now. Poor Mrs Murch is pretty well worn out. Cousin John was the only one looking anything like well. Hewitt arrived home in the evening.

Sunday 6th February

Hewitt went to Malvern for the day. I went to the Cathedral. In the evening Mac came in to tea with me and we agreed God willing our lives should some day be one though our prospects at present are hopeless. It is only changing what has been practically [going on *crossed out*] for nearly three years into actuality and I think will be better for both of us. Father and Mother and of course my near relations will have to be told but no one else on my side. I don't want congratulations to my face and then to have such remarks as "it's a poor look out" etc. when my back is turned. I am afraid that is what they would say. He is fonder of me but I would rather have it so and as he says, "it is all the better for me". I feel quite sure the more I know him the better I shall like him. He has been so good and patient with me when he has had no cause to be.

Monday 7th February

A nice bright day but very wet and dirty under foot so I went to see nobody and nobody came to see me but I had a busy day chip carving, working and reading so I did not find the time long.

Tuesday 8th February

Another quiet but pleasant day. Father came over to dine with us, left by the 5 train. I did not go out all day.

---

1   Clem Murch (22 at time of diary) son of John Murch who was nephew of William and Mary Chave (Flo's grandparents) – farmed Zeal Farm, Bampton in 1891. In 1902, the family lived at Huntington Court, Huntington.

2   Thomas Merson Murch was John's brother and died in 1898 aged 48.

Wednesday 9th February

Went to town in the afternoon. Called on the Davies[3] girls and invited them down Monday instead of Friday next, then called on the Mrs Davis,[4] Tanbrook, found it was her son's wedding day so Miss Davis was not at home.

Thursday 10th February

Hewitt and I started 10 a.m. for Malvern on our cycles. The roads were so dirty. We reached Malvern about 1 o'clock, left again at 3. Father and Mother walking up to the "Wych" with us. We got along alright until about 11 miles from home when I heard a slight explosion and thought my machine felt very bumpy, and getting off found my front tire quite soft. Hewitt tried to blow it up but in rain so there was nothing for it but to walk on to Ashperton a mile and a half and wait till 8.6 for a train or walk back 3 miles to Ledbury. By so doing we could catch a train an hour earlier so as it was only 5 o'clock we chose that course and reached home about 8 o'clock tired and hungry. We did enjoy our tea.

Friday 11th February

I had such a bad cold that I did not go out all day. Mrs Jackson called. Had afternoon tea with me and made friends with "Billie". They seemed mutually taken with each other and if I wanted to get rid of him she would be another candidate.

Saturday 12th February

Hewitt went to Birmingham for the afternoon, reached home in the early morning. I went in town, called on Mrs Moore.[5] Got my cycle. Was relieved to hear it was not a puncture but cut through in some way by the wire inside. Must have been badly put on. Poor Tom Murch died yesterday at 6 a.m.

---

3   Gertrude (28 yrs) and Mary (30 yrs) Davies. Probably the daughters of Thomas Davies, retired book seller living in Greyfriars Hotel.

4   Mrs Davis – Annie Davis (60 yrs), wife of Arthur D Davis, baker, lived at 90A Widemarsh St (near Tanbrook Villas) in 1901, with daughter Alice (39 yrs).

5   Mrs Moore (57 yrs), married to Dr Henry Moore (born Lucknow, India) 26 Broad Street, Hereford. Mother of Etta Baker.

Sunday 13th February

Hewitt and I both home all day. He was tired and it was so wet underfoot, I thought it was the best place for me too.

"Mac" at The Moor House, Hereford, circa 1895
Photo: Dr W A McCutchan

Flo at The Moor House, Hereford circa 1895.
Photo: Dr W A McCutchan

Monday 14th February

Did not go out all day. Hewitt went to Cardiff. Gertrude and Mary Davies came for the cycle ride but went for it by themselves. I felt so very tired that I cried off. They came back to tea and left about 6.50. I expect they thought

I was glad for them to go and so I was for I was expecting Mac and terribly afraid they would not be gone before he arrived. He spent about two hours with me. They have some theatricals on on Thursday to which he wants me to come. I want to go too if we can manage it. It will have to be done through Mrs Moore as I know Hewitt won't go. He thinks he ought to write to Father. I gave him permission.

Tuesday 15th February

Mother's birthday. I went to Malvern and spent the day with her. She had some nice presents. We bought her a very pretty table centre. Two new people, husband and wife, arrived. I left by the 5.20 train. Mother came to see me off. I told her the decision Mac and I had come to and asked her to tell Father. I could not screw up sufficient courage to tell them both.

It was not a very nice day, such a rough wind gave me a headache. Father had a donkey chair for an hour in the morning and Mother and I walked with him. Found Dr Morrison's invite on my return, also note from Etta asking if they could share a carriage with me so I went in by one bus and back in the next to tell her "yes". Also a note from Mrs Vevers asking me to tea that afternoon, and a letter from Evie asking me there Friday but I can't go as I had previously promised Mrs Moore.

Wednesday 16th February

Rode over to Huntington in the morning and paid my visit of condolence to Mrs Murch. Also called on Mrs Vevers as I was passing, to explain why I had not gone yesterday. In the afternoon rode in town and ordered a wreath and then called on Mrs Evans, Holmer.

Thursday 17th February

Mrs Moore and Etta called with the cab about 6 so we arrived in very good time. I enjoyed the "Babes in the Wood" very much. They acted it very well. Afterwards we had supper at Dr Morrison's. Mac was very quiet but Mrs Moore assured me he can talk, which of course was great news to me. I felt I was acting a part all the evening. Dr Morrison is going to London Sunday so I shall not be able to see Mac for some time.

Friday 18ᵗʰ February

A nasty snowy day so I did not go to Mrs Moore's or outside the door all day, but that was all the better for my work.

Saturday 19ᵗʰ February

Went in town in the morning. Called on Mrs Moore intending to have dinner there. However they didn't invite me so like a bad penny I had to return. Expected Mrs Murch in the afternoon but the post brought me a letter to say she couldn't come.

Dr Morrison's house at Burghill Asylum – now St Mary's Park, Burghill
Photo: Carol Parker

Sunday 20ᵗʰ February

Hewitt went to Malvern. Had a little snow in the afternoon. Australian letters arrived. Harold[6] did not sail in the Brittannia after all but said he should start without fail a fortnight later in the "Oceana".

---

6   Harold Chave (19 yrs) Flo's youngest brother

Monday 21st February

I went to Malvern by the 9.40 train. Father and Mother met me and we went for a walk and in the afternoon for a drive. Father had heard from Mac and they were both pleased with his letter. Thought it very well written. I think they are both rather afraid I've done it for the sake of matrimony as is every engagement. Hadn't that ulterior end in view but if that was my only motive poor me, what a forlorn hope! However, Father was very kind and said if Mac could find anything suitable he would help us to it by advancing some money. I can't wonder of course that they are not elated. Still I think I'm right. Time will shew and prove me so I trust. Willie Bond arrived in the afternoon, an ??absent visit as he returns Wednesday.

Tuesday 22nd February

Father and Willie came over to dinner and returned by 6 train. Flossie Clarkson[7] called in the morning asking me to go to the Marsh in the afternoon. My previous engagement prevented so I went for a ride round Credenhill with Flossie instead. Went to Mrs Vevers about 4. Had afternoon tea. Mrs Johnson and Evie Keay were there too.

Wednesday 23rd February

Called on Mrs Davis, Miss expected tomorrow. Then went on to the Ballards and had afternoon tea. Kitty was expecting her new cycle any moment and it arrived just as I left.

Thursday 24th February

Edith and I rode to the Marsh,[8] had our tea there and spent a pleasant afternoon. Got home just as it was getting dark.

Friday 25th February

Spent the afternoon at the Moores teaching Mrs Moore drawn thread work. Came home by the 8.5 bus. Mr Moore had a very bad cold.

---

7   Flossie Clarkson – probably Florence (25 yrs), daughter of Henry Clarkson, Grocer and wine Merchant, living at Bodenham Rd Crescent, Tupsley, Hereford in 1891. Sister of Edith Clarkson.

8   Possibly Wellington Marsh, north of Hereford.

Saturday 26th February

Mrs Lloyd and I rode out to Thowle and had afternoon tea. Roads pretty good until we got to the lane leading to the house which was very bad. Mac spent the evening with me.

Sunday 27th February

Hewitt went to Malvern in the morning. It was very wet about Church time so I did not go. Went in the afternoon about 4 to St John's instead. Mac came into tea with me and stayed till Hewitt's return.

Monday 28th February

Father came over for the day. I had quite a reception. First Alice Davis, then Mrs Jackson and Edith Clarkson. They had no sooner gone than Mac arrived, wanting to know if I could go to Malvern with him next day. Afterwards I walked up to Mrs Lloyd's to tell her I could not go for a ride on the morrow as we had arranged.

March 1898

Tuesday 1ˢᵗ March

Mac called for me about 11. It was pouring with rain, still we decided to venture as he had got the day off on purpose. It cleared off before we got there and after lunch we went to the top of the hill, had a snowstorm on the way and got back very late for tea, after which Mother and I went out in the town and Mac played billiards with Father. We left by the last train. It was pelting with rain when we reached Hereford so we had a cab back. Mac said he had enjoyed his day. I know I did but I think we both felt very tired. The wind was so strong up the hill.

Wednesday 2ⁿᵈ March

I expected Mrs Evans to tea but had a note saying she could not come so I spent a very quiet day indoors.

Friday 4ᵗʰ March

Tom[1] and I decided to ride to Malvern. Blowing up my tyre it burst so I had to take it into Howell's and borrow one from there and leave mine to be repaired. I did not like the exchange. Still I managed very well and we reached our destination about 1.30. They were rather surprised but very pleased to see us. We started back about 4 and got home at 7 without any misadventure. I was rather tired as we had done about 48 miles.

---

1   Tom Chave (24 at time of diary) Flo's younger brother. Later had doctor's practice in Cardiff. Married Florence Mairis, matron at Hereford Hospital.

Mr & Mrs W F Chave
[Courtesy of Sally McLean]

Dr H C Moore, stepfather of Flo's friend, Etta Baker, lived in No 26 Broad Street, Hereford, – the tall house on the right. It was demolished in 1935. Dr Moore was president of the Woolhope Club, of which William Chave was a member. Mrs Chave and her daughters would attend meetings.

[Photograph reproduced with kind permission of Herefordshire Libraries / herefordshirehistory.org.uk]

Saturday 5th March

The boys started for Leominster in the afternoon. I went in town and called on Etta. Mrs Moore was out. Etta was in bed but I went up and saw her and partook of afternoon tea. Mac came in the evening. The boys did not get back until 8.30 or 9 so we had a little time to ourselves.

Sunday 6th March

Church in the morning. Went to All Saints. It was snowing a little when I went but pouring with rain on my return. Rest of the day to myself. The boys had gone to Malvern. I expected Mac but he did not come.

7th March

Father came over. Tom and I met May Lang on her way to Sidmouth. Walked back round the town. Boys out all the evening, wish I had known they were going beforehand.

Tuesday 8th March

Went for a ride with Mrs Lloyd in the morning, only a short one. Went in town and called on Etta in afternoon. She was about again.

Wednesday 9th March

Father over to dinner. Hewitt and he going to Devon. I have to go to Malvern to keep Mother company. Tom and I rode to town in morning and I went to Malvern by an afternoon train.

Thursday 10th March

Mother and I went for a long walk to the Holy Well. Back to lunch. Tom turned up on his cycle. Took him round Ladies Walk in afternoon and he left about 4. Mother and I quite tired with our walking so much.

Friday 11th March

Explored another walk beyond the Holy Well and were very charmed with it. Rested after lunch. Went out after tea to meet Father at station. Looking very well.

Saturday 12th March

Mother and I to Cox and Painter's to choose a cycling dress. Expected Mac so met the 12.5 train but no Mac. Met the 1.42 and still he was not but the 3 train and 3rd time was lucky so took him for a walk. He had brought over some rings for me to see. I wanted one without any stone so that I can wear it always. I dislike the look of stones in the morning. Besides I need never take it off now until he is able to give me the one that is perfectly plain. This one will look very nice, I think, and being in form of a knot (a true lover's one I hope) is surely most applicable. I tell him he must give me a dress one when he is wealthy. We were late for tea purposely. It was so much nicer to ourselves. The gents played billiards afterwards until it was time for him to start to the station whither I accompanied him.

Sunday 13th March

Went to Emmanuel Church in morning. Hewitt arrived to lunch. Mother and I went to the Abbey in the evening.

Monday 14th March

Tried on my dress in morning. Returned to Hereford in afternoon. The boys were going to Leominster so Mac and I were going to have a nice tete a tete which was frustrated by Tom who was not feeling well so stayed at home. I should not have minded if the boys were kinder about him. Tom was very nice whilst he was here but after he had gone told me he was "dead alive" and he was very sorry but he didn't think much of him. I suppose they think I have no feeling but it hurts. Certainly I asked his opinion but I did not expect to be so wounded. Besides it frightens me for supposing they are right and I am wrong! Pray God it may not be so. They have not congratulated me either or for the matter of that him which at least they might have done for they do know a little bit about me. After all Ivy[2] was wise. The opinion of her relatives cannot wound her out there and that of strangers doesn't matter.

Tuesday 15th March

Father came over in the evening. I called on Mrs Lloyd and the Clarksons and Etta Baker. After dinner walked to Huntington with Father, then when

---

2   Ivy – Caroline Ivy Chave (23 yrs), Flo's younger sister, was married during the family's trip to Australia.

I had seen him and Tom off for Malvern, I called on the Walmsleys. Sarah was not home and Mrs was so busy with the packing up that I could not stay long. Then I went to the Ballards and had tea with Kitty who had just returned from Prior's Ct, and caught the 8.5 bus home.

Caroline "Ivy" Chave – circa 1895
Photo: Dr W A McCutchan

The Prell Family in Australia 1918
[Courtesy of Sally McLean]

Wednesday 16th March

Mr Broadley (L'land) was expected to lunch with Father so I went over by the 9.40 train. We took him for a nice drive round the British Camp and back through the "Wych". The day was so clear. It was beautiful. After dinner, the gents amused themselves with Billiards. I went to have my dress tried on. Afraid they are not going to make a great success of it. Mother came down to see me off and meet the Chaves who are paying Father a visit. It was just "how d'you do and goodbye."

Thursday 17th March

Cycled to Train Inn with Mrs Lloyd and Mr Jacob. It was hard work going being uphill nearly all the way and the wind against us and a very strong one; after dinner cycled up and enquired after Mrs Kay[3] and then had tea with the Davises. Miss Davis[4] is going to teach me Relief Carving. 1st lesson Saturday.

Friday 18th March

Was going to Malvern with Mrs Lloyd but the weather was not tempting, so windy. It went down a bit in the afternoon, so I cycled up to see her and had a cup of tea with them.

Saturday 19th March

Went early to Miss Davis to have my lesson and stayed there till the 6 bus. Got on fairly well. Mac came in the evening soon after I got back. Brought my ring which looks very nice but I don't want to wear it till I leave Hereford.

Sunday 20th March

Hewitt did not go to Malvern but went out so I was all alone all day, Mac even being too busy to come. I went to the Cathedral in the morning but did not care for the preacher one bit so did not enjoy the sermon.

---

3   Mrs Kay, possibly Sarah Jane Kay (56 at time of diary) living at Broughton House, Ledbury Rd. Husband, Edward, was Supervisor of Inland Revenue. They had 6 children, one of whom would die aged 19 in 1898.

4   Miss Davis – Alice Davis (39 yrs) daughter of Arthur and Annie Davis.

Monday 21st March

This terrible day will ever stand out in my mind. I went to Miss Barker's recital with Mrs Lloyd, went back with her to afternoon tea and then went in and had tea with Etta. I had told Hewitt I meant to do so and just as I was about to leave, a note came to me from him saying "Come at once by cab important", and getting back found I had to go at once to Malvern to break the sad news to my dear parents that our darling Harold would never return to us having died at sea March 11th of acute inflammation of the lungs. It was the hardest task I have ever had to do in my life. They bore it very bravely but the trial is so bitter. We were expecting and so looking forward to seeing him Saturday or Sunday next. A letter from the "Oceana" doctor and purser told us.

Tuesday 22nd March

We spent a long almost sleepless night and a dreary day. Dear old Hewitt came over in the afternoon. We went for a drive but time passed slowly. Everyone was very kind to us in the hotel. Mother thought she would rather go out in the evening to hear Mark Guy Pearse[5] lecture on the West End of London so I went with her. I'm afraid we both wished we had stayed at home. It was too painful (being slightly humorous) for anyone in trouble such as ours.

Wednesday 23rd March

Brought us a letter from the steward who had nursed our dear one to the last. He was only laid up a week but when he saw the doctor it was too late. Nothing could be done for him. He died at 6.30 in the morning and they buried him in the Red Sea at 8.30. Father and Mother, Ivy and I have much to be thankful for in the remembrance of the last two years we spent with our darling. He was so unselfish and loving to us all. God help me to follow his example. I came back to Hereford in the afternoon and met Edith Clarkson at the station. She walked home with me, waited whilst I had some tea and walked in town with me afterwards as I was obliged to go to see Mrs Moore. It was good of Edith. I shall not soon forget her kindness to me. Found Mac on my return. It was good of him to come. He had only heard of our trouble accidentally in the morning.

---

5   Mark Guy Pearce (1842-1930) Cornish Methodist preacher, and highly popular
     lecturer and author.

Thursday 24th March

Went over to Malvern by 12.45 train. There were many kind sympathetic letters but they were very painful to read. Dear old Mac wanted to show his sympathy with Father and Mother so came over by the 4 train to fetch me. It was such a nasty cold damp day. I did appreciate his kindness though I'm afraid he could not have thought so. I felt so miserable just as if my heart was dead so I must have been a wretched companion. We returned by the 7.10 train.

Friday 25th March

Did not go out till evening. Tom[6] came over so walked with him to the station to meet Mabel but only had time for a glimpse of her as she and Tom went on to Malvern by next train.

Saturday 26th March

Went to Malvern by 9.40 train. A bitterly cold day. No-one met me. Tom,[7] Cecil and Ernest Chave[8] went to London as the "Oceana" was expected Sunday. Mother, May and I went to the dressmaker. Hewitt came over by the afternoon train.

Sunday 27th March

Went to the Priory in the morning. It was wet. The service was nice and the text was "leaving (or forgetting) those things which are behind, I press forward." Hewitt, Mother and I went to Emmanuel in the evening.

Monday 28th March

Hewitt returned. We walked down to the station to see him off and then walked round the College way home. In the afternoon, Mother and Mabel went for a walk and Father, Mrs Hollingsworth, Miss Watson, a very "nice Irish girl" and I went for a drive.

---

6   Tom Chave, i.e. Flo's younger brother.

7   Ditto.

8   2Cecil (27 yrs) and Ernest Chave (28 yrs) – sons of John Anstey Chave, brother of Flo's father. Born in Hillingdon, Middx, Cecil was living with sister, Evelyn, in Westminster in 1901.

Tuesday 29ᵗʰ March

Mabel left us. We walked down and saw her off. It was not a very nice day. My cycling dress which has been back two or three times is still a non-success. I was just putting on my veil after afternoon tea to go and complain about it again when a young lady came from Cox and Painter's to enquire if it was a success and today if it wasn't they would take it back and make me a new one. So I said I was unable to call it a success and would come about it next morning.

Wednesday 30ᵗʰ March

Went to Cox and Painter's in the morning and chose a ready made coat and skirt which they said they could alter to fit me. I prefer the material to the original so hope this time it will be a success. It is more expensive too. Tom came back by the 5 o'clock train. He could not tell us much more about our dear one but he had seen the purser, doctor and steward and thought they had done all they could for dear Harold's comfort. He was unconscious for the last three days and must have been quite unlike himself the whole way as he never entered into any of the games but seemed to lie about in his deck chair all day.

Thursday 31ˢᵗ March

Father had a donkey to the top of the hill. The rest of us walked. Hewitt came in the afternoon and I returned with him I the evening to Hereford. Tom brought us back some bad news. Yesterday he had met ?Willie and Edward in London, Alphie had gone out of his mind and they had had to admit him into a private asylum. They do seem to have more than their share of trouble. We took a walk through the Ladies Walk in the afternoon.

April 1898

Friday 1st April

Alice Davis came to see me in the morning. I also saw Mrs Evans for a few minutes as she was catching a bus. Mrs Lloyd came to afternoon tea and after she left I walked in town, came home to tea and walked in again to post a letter to Father

Saturday 2nd April

Tom came over to lunch. Edward came by the 2.15 train. They walked in town with me and I called to see Mrs Jackson. She had been to see me whilst I was away. She was very nice to me and walked nearly all the way home with me. She really seemed to feel very deeply our loss. Mac came in the evening. The boys went to the station to see Tom off, for which we were not sorry.

Sunday 3rd April

Went to church in morning. Saw Etta and she and Mrs Moore walked nearly all the way home with me. Mac came to tea with me. He was not looking very well but did not complain.

Monday 4th April

Busy morning marking out a pattern on an afternoon tea cloth and doing a little carving. Spent the afternoon having a lesson at Miss Davis.

Tuesday 5th April

Tom cycled over in the morning and I cycled back with him in the afternoon. It was an ideal afternoon for cycling but I got very tired before we reached our journey's end.

Wednesday 6th April

Spent the day writing letters and sending off our cards of thanks. It was a sad task and I was very thankful when it was over. Father went over to Hereford.

Thursday 7th April

Mabel and Aunt Elise came, also Edward and Hewitt so we are a good party of ourselves. Tom went over to Hereford in the afternoon to see if our dear one's things were according to the Inventory.

Friday 8th April

Good Friday. We are a crowd. Such a lot of new faces. It was a lovely day but too gusty and dusty to be pleasant walking. We went to church in the morning and spent the rest of the day indoors.

Saturday 9th April

My birthday. I had such nice presents – nearly all in the leather line. A beautiful dressing case from Mabel, Tom and Hewitt, and a cash box equally nice from Aunt Sophie and Aunt Elise, a prayer and hymn book in case from Rose and a hat from Father and Mother. Mother also gave me dear Harold's matchbox which will of course always be very valuable to me. Mother, Mabel and Aunt went for a long walk in the afternoon. I took Miss Gilbert for a short one, Miss Watson (my favouriter [sic]) being laid up with a bad ancle [sic]

Sunday 10th April

Easter Sunday. Bad news greeted me, poor old Mac being laid up with influenza. It makes me feel very anxious. Such a wet morning. Did not go to church. It was such a long day. I was glad when it was over.

Monday 11th April

I worked all morning, others walked, and played croquet. Afternoon and evening very wet, most unfortunate for a Bank Holiday.

Wednesday 13th April

Went to Miss Davis for another lesson and after tea we walked in town and brought my tools and a table to operate on. Mother had arrived before I returned.

Thursday 14th April

Mother and I spent a busy day. In the morning went through dear Harold's clothes and in the afternoon went to Huntington and went through all the cases we had stored there to pick up and pack the things we needed as we have to provide our own plate and linen at Hele. I felt much better and brighter. Yesterday I was very miserable. I had not heard how Mac was going on and could not go and enquire, and I felt altogether wretched. I had a letter by this evening post saying he was convalescing rapidly. I was very thankful to receive it – it was a great relief.

Friday 15th April

Mother and I picked up our old clothes and I walked in town to request Miss O'Hare to come and her parents were quite willing for her to go with us as she will be ready to accompany us on Tuesday. I am glad as we had not anyone in view. She seems a nice child, has grown very like Annie and will, I think suit us very nicely.

Saturday 16th April

A very busy morning packing my Saratoga as all the heavy luggage had to be sent off this afternoon. Miss Davis came to give me my final lesson.

Sunday 17th April

Went to St Peter's Church. Hewitt cycled to Malvern. Tom returned with him about 7 o'clock. He was going down to Devon by the next train. He had only just time to have his tea and change his costume before he was off again.

Monday 18th April

Went up to Mrs Lloyd's on my cycle but we did not go for a ride. I was not sorry for I had a dreadful cold yesterday and it was still bad. Was very sorry on picking up the paper to see that Mr Crotty had died on the 16th. Nellie's funeral is this afternoon at 2 o'clock. Tom will be there as that was why he went to Devon. I am so sorry for them. They go to Exeter for the night and return to Culcheth[1] tomorrow. I rode to Huntington in the afternoon to go through a chest and drawers. It did not take too long and then I returned and went to bed till tea time.

Culcheth Hall School, Altrincham, opened 1891 with Ivy Chave a pupil there. Run by Mrs Chave's nieces, the Misses Lang.

Photo: Philip Hodges [Courtesy of Bowdon Preparatory School]

St Michael's Chapel, Chapel Hill, Torquay

Photo: J L Parton [Wikipedia]

1   Culcheth – Culcheth Hall School, Bowden, run by the Misses Lang.

April 1898 continued

Flo, Mabel and their parents go to stay in Hele, Devon, in a house Mr Chave has bought. Hele is just south of Cullompton and about 20 miles south of Cove where Flo's cousins live.

Tuesday 19ᵗʰ April

Spent a very busy morning packing. Met Father and Mother and Mabel at 12 o'clock. Mr Jones and Minnie were there in good time. We had a quiet journey and not such a trying one as we expected and ourselves and luggage arrived quite safely at Hele about five. Garrish the gardener was there to meet us and he had aired all the blankets and the rooms so we were able to get our tea at once as Mother had brought some provisions, and then make the beds and do a little unpacking. It was very nice being able to spend the night there instead of going to an hotel. We like the place. It has a pretty bit of garden. The house is nicely furnished and good rooms, the only drawback is the kitchen which is downstairs.

Wednesday 20ᵗʰ April

A very wet day but we were so busy unpacking that we had not time to mind much – Minnie is a treasure. We should have had to work hard if we had not had her there as a lot of dusting to be done. The dog "Tiger" is a hideous looking animal though very different from his name apparently. The gardener seems very proud of his garden. I certainly never have seen more lovely violets.

Thursday 21ˢᵗ April

Mother and Mabel explored Bradninch in the morning and took a long walk again in the afternoon. Minnie also took a walk with Mrs Garrish. I stayed at home and wrote letters. I was relieved at getting Mac's this morning as I did not see or hear anything of him before leaving. He had found writing even too great an effort. We had a caller in the evening, Mr Scott Smith through whom Father bought the place. We cannot hear of another girl, not one to be got about this part. They all work at the paper mill. Our work not being enough. One of the …must smoke so terrifically that the hall and staircase landing were covered with smut in the morning.

Friday 22nd April

Had to have quite a small spring clean before breakfast. Father, Mother and Mabel went to Exeter for the afternoon so we had an early lunch.

Saturday 23rd April

Hewitt arrived in the morning. Tom, Edward and Willie cycled over, the other two by train. Tom stayed with us. We went for a walk in the evening. Tom and I went along the road to Plymtree. It was a long time since he and I had had a walk alone together

Sunday 24th April

All went to church in morning except Minnie and I – we stayed home to cook the dinner. Afternoon Mother, Tom and Mabel walked to stoke and back. I was dreadfully tired all day and did not go out at all.

Monday 25th April

Edward, Rose and Henry cycled over for the day. Very glad to see them all, especially Rose. Ali,[2] his wife and two children are with them at Cove. After they left the others except Mabel went for a walk. Hewitt left in the afternoon.

Tuesday 26th April

Mabel and I cycled into Cullompton and back before dinner. After tea they all took a walk to Bradninch (I was going to Torquay today but had a letter from Mac saying he could not get away that day). Their walk resulted in a girl being found. They acted on "when in doubt ask a policeman", and he told them of one so they went, saw and engaged her and she comes Thursday. I am glad for Minnie's sake. It is so lonely for the child.

Wednesday 27th April

A very nice letter from Mrs Crotty in answer to mine. Tom and Mabel left. We were sorry to see them go. Father went to Exeter. Such a sad accident. The young fellow who helped bring up our luggage was killed last night –

---

2   Alfred Bond (33 yrs) 2nd son of Flo's Aunt Anna and brother to Willie, Edward, Rose and Henry, living at Collipriest Farm, Lowman, Tiverton in 1871

he was passing by some place near where there was a fire and went to save someone, and the roof fell on him. He leaves a wife and one child, and there will not be another.

Thursday 28th April

Postcard from Tom and letter from Hewitt which said he had seen Mac and he was going to Torquay today so I expected a wire all day but it didn't come. Mary arrived about 6 but I did not see her till next morning.

Friday 29th April

Like her look. She seems to take right end of things. Heard from Mac. He comes tomorrow. Edward and I went into Exeter by market train. I returned by 11.40. Edward went home. Mother and I walked to Bradninch in the evening.

Saturday 30th April

Busy morning in kitchen, packed in afternoon. Letter from Mac saying he might not be able to come. Would telegraph if he couldn't. Just as I thought I was safe and was busy packing, a wire arrived. I was much relieved on opening it to find it said he was starting. I went in [to Torquay] by the 4.48. His train was very late but we met all right and found Aunt Sophie awaiting us. They had two visitors staying with them, Miss Vowler and Mrs Pavey (a friend of Anna's). The ordeal went off very well and we had a game of whist in the evening. After supper Mac and I retired to the dining room to have a smoke and chat.

May 1898

Sunday 1st May

Mac and I went to All Saints to church. The afternoon we spent in the dining room which the rest most kindly gave up to us. The day was very wet so we did not go to church in the evening but it cleared off about 7.30 so Mac and I just went down to see the sea and get a whiff of fresh air.

Monday 2nd May

We went down to see the town and the sea wall and hear the band play. Aunt Sophie took us a very nice drive in the afternoon round the "New Cut", "Anstey Cove", and "Babbacombe". Aunt Elise left us in the morning for Hele. Evening, Mac did not care for further walking. I thought he might like a change of girls as he had seen pretty much of me so left him in the drawing room with Miss Vowler and talked to Aunt Sophie in the dining room.

Tuesday 3rd May

Took Mac round the Rosary Greenhouses and then up Chapel Hill and back to see the Rock Walk. He is a very interesting companion – so observant and seems so fond of the birds. He notices things I should never see. We left by the 3.26 train for Hele. Met Father on the Exeter platform. Got home just in time for tea, after which we all walked down to the station to see Aunt Elise off as she returned to Torquay and took my cycle with her to have it cleaned for me. Whist in the evening. Mac and I had the luck.

The Gables, North Street,
Stoke under Ham – 1890–95
Photo: Dr W A McCutchan

Dr McCutchan at the Gables – 1890–95
Photo: Dr W A McCutchan

Wednesday 4th May

Such a strange coincidence. When Mother went down to the kitchen, our new girl, Mary (her real name is Ellen) said, "I know that gentleman who came last night. His name is Dr McCutchan. I used to live with Mr Walters[1] where he was assistant at Stoke."

She gave him a very good character to Mother. The people at Stoke thought a great deal of him. He was greatly beloved and was so good to the poor, did more for them really than he could afford, and all about his testimonial. She said she knew him at once when she saw him and said to herself, "if Miss Florrie's engaged to him she will have a good husband." She told me the people had a very warm heart for him somehow and showed me some photos she was treasuring up that he had given her.

I was so glad about it, more glad than I can say for Father and Mother to have such unsolicited testimony to his worth for I have always had a feeling that they all think I have made a mistake. I suppose as long as I don't it doesn't much matter. Still I would rather that they appreciate him.

He seems rather clever with his hands for which I am very glad. He mended up an old chair for us very nicely. We only went out in the garden and sauntered about in the morning and we expected Edward Chave[2] and Willie Bond to dinner but had a wire from them saying they couldn't come which was very nice for Mac and me as the drawing room fire had been lighted in their honour. We were able to sit by it in the afternoon.

He gave me my ring which I like very much. I meant to have had it before leaving Hereford, but was unable as I could not see him. It looked like a case of "he who will not when he may". He gave me another little one too. Also a knot one of my own is too big for me so he thought that one would just keep it on and so it does. He had to leave by the 11.48 train. I was sorry to see him go.

I think he will make me very happy if fortune will only favour him in the way of a berth. Father and Mother took a walk in the evening. Ellen was out so I had to stay home with Minnie.

---

1   Mr Walters – Dr Walter Winter Walter – Mac worked for him as Medical Assistant in Stoke sub Hamdon from 1890 to 1894.

2   Edward Chave (45 at time of diary) son of WFC's brother, Edward. Farmed at Widhayes, Uplowman.

Thursday 5ᵗʰ May

Such a wet day. No going outside the door. Spent the morning machining and the afternoon writing letters, evening playing "euchre".

Friday 6ᵗʰ May

Mother took me such a long walk. It was a lovely morning but tiring for walking. We meant to go to Silverton but never got there. Edward Chave came in the afternoon. Brought us more bad news. Edward Bond had been thrown out of his trap carriage, smashed to atoms. He could not tell us how Edward fared. It made us feel very anxious. Clem Murch came up and spent the evening.

Saturday 7ᵗʰ May

A letter from Edw. Chave³ saying Edward progressing satisfactorily. A bad cut at back of head and a bruise on the forehead. Willie also telegraphed, "Danger over". It was a great relief to us. Morning machining. Father went to Exeter in afternoon.

Sunday 8ᵗʰ May

Rather damp so Mother and I went to church by ourselves. It is a funny little chapel of ease, looks as if it had been converted out of a house. The curate played the harmonium as well as did the service. It was a funeral one so very painful to us. I don't think I shall ever like the hymn, "Thy will be done" in church again. Stayed home the rest of the day.

Monday 9ᵗʰ May

A lovely morning. I have a little room that is not wanted for my sanctum. It is so nice as I can do my carving, painting etc without interruption. We had a quiet day. Father and Mother took a stroll in the evening. The great event of the day was giving the dog a wash. It did him a lot of good and he took it very well.

Tuesday 10ᵗʰ May

Busy morning in the kitchen. Mother walked to Bradninch. The Australian letters came. They were very sad, being the first we have had from Ivy after

---

3   Edw. Chave – probably his father, Edward Chave born Uplowman ca 1816.

she had heard of our loss. Mrs Franklyn and Miss Vowler called in the afternoon. Evening we took a walk.

Wednesday 11th May

Much as usual – a lovely day.

Thursday 12th May

Dreamt a nice dream about our dear old Harold. Saw him so plainly as I have so often seen him with his arm round Mother's neck. We seemed to have heard of his death and then gone on a boat and there we met him. He had been very ill but had recovered. It was sad to wake and find it only a dream. Spent a quiet day. Went for a walk round Killerton after tea with Father and Mother.

Friday 13th May

Mother and I called on the Crossleighs. They seemed to have a pretty garden but we did not see them as the servant said "Not at home". The day was very showery. Mrs Lloyd arrived safely and we all took a walk after tea.

Saturday 14th May

Cycled to Exeter. It was a lovely day and we quite enjoyed our day. We had a couple of hours there, saw the Cathedral and shops and returned round Stoke and Killerton. We went through Broadclyst and Pinhoe.

Sunday 15th May

All went to church but me. I did not feel at all well but went for a walk in the evening with Mrs Lloyd. We found the sweetest little bird's nest with five eggs in.

Monday 16th May

Took train to Totnes, from there up the Dart to Dartmouth. Thence train to Torquay where we took tea at Bean Coin, as usual found them a housefull. Mrs Pavey still there and Ali, his wife and children. First time I have seen him since he went to Australia.

Tuesday 17th May

We cycled to Cove, had a lovely ride there but it came on to rain and rained all the afternoon and evening so we had to leave our cycles there and return by train. The boy had to meet Willie so drove us to Bampton Station. There we had to wait three quarters of an hour. When we got to Tiverton, we had to sit half an hour in a waiting room without a fire or lamp, then we had to change at Tiverton Junction and wait twenty minutes but the climax was reached when we got to Hele and found ourselves bolted out. They had quite given us up, but luckily had not gone to bed. We shook Garrish's garden door and shouted but all to no purpose. At last Mr ?Alno's son heard us and came out to enquire. He got over a low wall and let us in, and then our difficulties for that night were over.

Wednesday 18th May

We took the train for Exe Valley to Bampton. Walked from there to Cove. Spent a pleasant afternoon there and then cycled home. Willie and Rose accompanying us a good part of the way.

Thursday 19th May

Wet and rough. Not out all day. Very lucky we went to Cove yesterday. Ascension Day. Gladstone died.

Friday 20th May

Went a short walk in the morning. The evening turned out very wet again.

Saturday 21st May

Went to Torquay by excursion, arrived in good time for dinner. Afternoon did not look very tempting but we took our teas and went to Anstey's Cove. Were rewarded with a lovely evening. Walked home the New Cut to Daddy Hole and St John's Wood.

Sunday 22nd May

Went to church. Had rather a funeral sermon and then the Dead March. It was too much for me. I had to leave the church. Mrs Lloyd made a very good dinner so decided to miss our tea, walked to Watcombe and back across the cliffs, a lovely walk. We took four hours but enjoyed it.

Monday 23rd May

We went by train to Lustleigh. Aunt Sophie and Alphie accompanied us. We walked up the Cleeve and had lunch there, then walked it to Becky Falls. Such a hot day and a stiff climb but lovely views. We had tea at the latter place. A coach and four arrived just as we were leaving. We were able to get seats on it so were spared the five miles of road for which we were very thankful. We got back to Torquay and had a nice tea and rest and then caught our train back to Hele. Etta had duly arrived in the afternoon. The Bonds had also cycled over but were gone before we arrived.

Tuesday 24th May

Mrs Lloyd left. Mother and I saw her off and that was all the outing we got, for the rest of the day was very wet.

Wednesday 25th May

Floods of rain at Tiverton yesterday. Did good bit of damage. Mother and Etta went to Bradninch in the morning. Tom arrived 4.48.

Thursday 26th May

Mother, Tom, Etta and I went a very pretty walk in the afternoon. Then all went down to meet Hewitt's train but only met his dog. He cycled from Exeter and arrived weary and worn, had taken wrong road and got into dreadful laver and had to walk most of the way.

Friday 27th May

Etta and I went to Exeter, enjoyed it very much. Returned by the 3 train. Tom's birthday. We gave him an umbrella. Father and Hewitt also went to town. They purchased a croquet set.

Saturday 28th May

Mother, Etta and I walked to Bradninch in the morning. Afternoon was devoted to croquet. I had a very bad cold all day so was glad to go early to bed.

Sunday 29th May

Whit Sunday. Went to church in the morning. Mother and I stayed Communion. Hewitt cycled to Cove after dinner, did not return. Etta and I were so cold in the afternoon we had to retire to the kitchen. Mother and Etta went to Bradninch Church in the evening.

Monday 30th May

Rather busy as May had a holiday and went to Plymouth for the day. Rose and Edward Bond cycled back with Hewitt. Arrived just as we were in the midst of dinner. Left soon after tea. Hewitt had a telegram to tell him poor old Mrs Beck had died 2.30 that afternoon and he went into Tiverton by train to let her brother know. Poor May arrived about 12 pm. When they got to Exeter they made them get out of the train and then told them there was no train on to Hele that night so the poor things had had to hire from Exeter and pay 15/- for it. May says no more excursions for her. She has finished up with them.

Tuesday 31st May

Aunt Elise and Carrie Langdon arrived in the morning. They had cycled to the Tremletts the evening before. Weather was so bad they trained to us and stayed the night. Mr & Mrs Baxeter came to tea. It was not at all a nice day, wet at least stormy. Tom left us by the 3.33.

June 1898

Wednesday 1st June

Hewitt, Aunt and Carrie left by same train. A very stormy morning. We walked to Bradninch, Father, Mother, Etta and I in the afternoon. Got caught in several storms. Evening was very wet.

Thursday 2nd June

A really nice day. Father and Mother went to Exeter after an early dinner and called on the Tremletts on their way home. Etta and I went a short cycle ride to Killerton, going one way and returning the other. Evening, we all went for a lovely walk, the same one that Mrs Lloyd and I went that Sunday. I was astonished at Father even attempting it for it was very hilly but he never even murmured.

Friday 3rd June

Nice letter from Mac. He hopes to have his holidays within a fortnight. Mother, Etta and I took our dinners and went on a ferning expedition but no sooner had we partaken of our repast than it poured with rain and we had to retrace our steps. Father went to Exeter, came back by 3 train, evening played "whist".

Saturday 4th June

Etta left by 10.13 train to Torquay. Father, Mother and I were just about to start for a walk in the evening when Willie Bond arrived. He had cycled over and cycled back, our walk could not come off.

Sunday 5th June

Church in the morning. Read in the afternoon and ?whist in the evening and a short walk for the dog's benefit, but after all he declined to accompany us.

Monday 6th June

Spent the morning painting. Afternoon Mother and I called on the Smiths. Etta returned in the evening.

Tuesday 7th June

All went for a walk in the morning but me. I wanted to paint. Afternoon Etta, Mother and I called on Mrs Duncan, the doctor's wife. Miss Smith was also there and a Mrs G Drew. Evening, croquet was the order of affairs.

Wednesday 8th June

Willie and Rose cycled over unexpectedly after dinner en route for Pinhoe, so they left soon after. We amused ourselves with croquet which it was too hot to enjoy much. Evening we all took a stroll.

Thursday 9th June

Father went a drive to taste some cider. Mother, Etta and I went for such a long walk. We all did ourselves up and were fit for nothing. The rest of the day we went to find Paradise but did not succeed.

Friday 10th June

Etta's last day so she devoted the afternoon to croquet. In the evening we all walked to Bradninch. Father and I went one way and Mother and Etta the other. They arrived first. A note from Mac. The committee has been. Praised him up. For which takes pleasure. He hopes to come the 23rd.

Saturday 11th June

Etta, Minnie and I went to Teignmouth. It was Minnie's first sight of the sea and it looked lovely. We had a nice day but decidedly too hot. Etta then went on to Torquay and Minnie and I returned to Hele. A man brought a pretty little pony for Father to see in the evening. I think very likely we shall

Mrs Caroline Chave, Flo's mother, The Moor House circa 1895
Photo: W A McCutchan

Flo Chave in the garden of The Moor House circa 1895
Photo: W A McCutchan

have it. The man said it was a "very loving little pony". It seems very quiet. I thought it was a large donkey when I went out first.

Sunday 12th June

A very quiet day. Church in the morning. A very nice sermon on Nicodemus by Mr Atherton. Rest of the day read.

Monday 13th June

Father and Mother and I had a very early lunch then they went to Hemyock to see a pony that was on offer. I stayed home and read and wrote. They returned ?4.48. Had had a wasted journey. Pony not for sale. Mother and I walked to the farm after tea to pay the milk bill.

Tuesday 14th June

Father and I devoted the afternoon to croquet. We had to have a fire. It was such a cold day. Evening Father and Mother walked to Bradninch. I had a practice.

Wednesday 15th June

Father and Mother went to Torquay. The former to attend a sale at Kingskerswell. They left by the 10.13 and returned by the 8.40 so I had a long day to myself which I spent in reading, writing and practising.

Thursday 16th June

Cycled by myself in the morning to invite the Tremletts to tea on Tuesday. Quite enjoyed the ride. It was a lovely morning. The afternoon was spent in needlework and the evening in croquet.

Friday 17th June

Went to Exeter with Father in the morning. We all took a stroll in the evening.

Saturday 18th June

Minnie went to a fete at Bradninch. Father and I spent the afternoon in croquet and Father and Mother took a stroll after tea.

Sunday 19th June

Church in the morning – a very nice sermon from Mr Atherton, rest of day read.

Monday 20th June

Aunt Sophie came. Arrived just in time for dinner. Hele was quite lively it being market day. Father saw Mr Hann and invited him into dinner. He came. Father went to a sale at Bradninch to buy a pony but it was bought in so he returned. William – the loving little pony – he did not think handsome enough. I wish he could have bought the other. It was a smart, pretty little turn out altogether. Mother and Aunt took a walk whilst Father and I had our usual contest.

Tuesday 21st June

Mac comes Thursday. The Tremletts came and spent the afternoon in croquet. They meant to go by 7 train but missed it so stayed till 10.

Wednesday 22nd June

Another pony came for inspection. Father is going to have it on appro.

Thursday 23rd June

Father and I drove over to Mr Baxter's. A nice going pony. Mother had a drive in the afternoon. Mac came in the evening. He is looking stronger and may be able to stay till 27th.

Friday 24th June

Father took Mac for a drive in the morning and I took him one in the afternoon. He took a snapshot or two.

Saturday 25th June

Busy fitting up the dark room. Stormy morning but cleared in the afternoon so Mac and I went a walk and took some more snapshots.

Sunday 26th June

Went to church in the morning and heard the late vicar Rev Capel Cull/ Cole? liked him very much. Mac and I went to Bradninch in the evening and heard him again. I did not like the sermon as well. Mac liked it better. Father offered £16 for the pony which was not accepted.

Monday 27th June

Mac left his machine yesterday so we walked in and fetched it. Mr Short the sexton showed us over the church and amused us very much – the screen is very curious. In the afternoon all of us went to the Tremletts. Went over the paper mills and had an enjoyable time, returning by the train.

Tuesday 28th June

Aunts and Mother to Tiverton early in the morning. Returned by 4.48. Busy doing up the dark room.

Flo with Mr &Mrs Chave (right) and Flo's ?aunts
Photo: Dr W A McCutchan

Ladies cycling group – photograph from the Chave records at Hereford Archives
– sadly without names.

[By kind permission of HARC]

Wednesday 29th June

Etta Baker returned to Hereford. Mac and I met her at Exeter, took in her
cycle for her. Afterwards went and inspected the town. Very hot and tired
we got so returned by the 5 train.

Thursday 30th June

Aunt Sophie, Father and Mother took train to Silverton, and Mac and I
rode and we went over the house called "Egremont Folly", a remarkable
old place seemingly built without rhyme or reason. The old house was not
bad but he seems to have built a new one all round it. The exterior is a very
grand one. The interior has never been finished as it would take another
£100,000 to finish it.

July 1898

Friday 1st July

Finished the dark room and now it is a "really" good one. Mother and Aunt Sophie spent the day in Exeter. Hewitt rode down on his cycle. Had had a hard day's work and arrived with a puncture and a broken lamp. Edward Bond came with him so far as ? *[illegible]*

Sat 2nd July

Another pony on appro. Father and Hewitt drove it about in the morning and Hewitt took Mother for a drive in the afternoon. It was a sweet looking little Exmoor but the verdict was "lazy" so it was returned and we are still without. Aunt Elise arrived late at night. Tom had cycled back with them and gone on to Cove with Rose. They seem to have enjoyed themselves. Willie and Edward cycled over in the morning and spent the day.

Sunday 3rd July

Mac and I went for a long walk. In the evening Father and Hewitt stayed home and Mother and aunts went to church.

Monday 4th July

Aunt, Mac and I rode into Exeter. A lovely morning. We enjoyed the ride. Had dinner there. Met Tom and Edward in there. They returned to Cove for dinner. Miss Luget rode back with us. She and Aunt reached Hele before us a good bit for Mac's machine went wrong. It was a pity for we had had such a nice day. Aunt and I rode as far as Broadclyst with Miss Luget after tea.

Tuesday 5th July

Mac went in with his cycle in the morning and Aunt Elise and I rode to Silverton to order some strawberries for the picnic tomorrow. In the afternoon Mother and Aunts went to Mrs Franklin's.

Wednesday 6th July

A delightful day. We had to leave Hele at 6.30. The Bradninch bus conveyed us to Stoke Canon where we caught the train to Dulverton. The Bonds and Tom meeting us there. Then we drove in a coach and four over the Moor to Cloutshaw where we had a sumptuous lunch of which we were greatly in need. Rambled about in the glen afterwards, driving back over Dunkery Beacon having had a most enjoyable picnic.

Thursday 7th July

Mr Reed sent word the other day that Father should have the pony for £16, none of the others we had in view did Father. Mother walked into Bradninch to say he would have it so "Polly" arrived in the afternoon and Father took Aunt Sophie for a drive.

Friday 8th July

Edward and Tom cycled over to dinner about 4. Aunt Elise and I cycled to Exeter going to Digby to see Grace.[1] It was a sad visit. She was not so well as I expected. Afterwards we went into Exeter to meet Mac who had come in by train to fetch his cycle and ride home with us. We went and had some tea and then started, Aunt Elise going on in front to call on the Tremletts. Just before we reached Cowley Bridge, Mac had a puncture and had to return to St David's. I thought he had just time to catch the train. I was obliged to go on because of Aunt. I found her almost tired of waiting and we rode home but found no Mac on our arrival, and poor fellow never got here till 11 o'clock.

He had arrived at the station just in time to see the train go out. Then he had walked up to the cycle shop and got the cycle repaired. Then when he got as far as Stoke Mills it gave out again and he had to walk all the rest of the way home. I was thankful to see him arrive. I thought he had met with

---

1   Grace. Identity not known, but the Exeter City Asylum was at Digby, Exeter.

an accident or lost his way. Aunt Sophie and Aunt Elise very kindly sat up with me.

Saturday 9ᵗʰ July

Father and Mother drove to Exeter and back. Aunt Elise cycled back to Torquay. Willie and Edward Bond called in and had a bit of lunch. Aunt Sophie left at 3. Miss Smith came to tea.

Sunday 10ᵗʰ July

Church in the morning. Mr Moseley preached. Mac and I spent a very quiet but happy day.

Monday 11ᵗʰ July

Mac and I had an early cup of tea and went off to Torquay by 1ˢᵗ train. Had another breakfast there on our arrival, then went in town, inspected the shops, back to dinner, then we all drove to Anstey's Cove and had tea returning to the station and home by last train after a very pleasant day.

Tuesday 12ᵗʰ July

Afternoon drove Mac to Stoke Canon to see the window in the church. Had a nice drive returning round Poltimore.

Wednesday 13ᵗʰ July

Miss Smith called in the morning to invite me up in the afternoon but I could not go as we were expecting Mrs Franklyn and Miss Brown. They came but didn't stay very late.

Thursday 14ᵗʰ July

Mac and I had a nice quiet day to ourselves. Father and Mother drove to Cove for the day at about 9 and got home about 8.30. Tom returned with them on his cycle. We had no interruption except Ed. Chave for an hour in the afternoon. Spent the day chiefly in photographic work. Mac has to go to London to take charge of a patient so has to leave tomorrow instead of Saturday.

Friday 15th July

Father went into Exeter by train. We had early lunch and then I drove Mac into Exeter to catch his train which ran through to London without stopping. I was sorry for him to go and so I think was he but the best of friends must part. He has another week in a month or so which we mean to spend at Torquay. Father returned with me. Ed Bond was here for the night.

Saturday 16th July

Edward left very early so I did not see him. He has gone back to Hereford. I did some needlework – quite a long time since I did any before. The pony had to rest.

Sunday 17th July

Went to church in the morning so hot coming home and terribly hot day. Father and Mother went for a stroll in the evening.

Monday 18th July

A quiet day. Father and Tom went a drive. Mother and I worked and read and I watched Tom ?? and fix his prints.

Tuesday 19th July

Tom and I cycled to Cove. Spent a pleasant day with Rose. Reached home about 9. Found Mr & Mrs Sawton had arrived.

Wednesday 20th July

I drove Tom to the Exeter Station per up the house and called on Miss Luget. Father came in by train, met me there and we had a pleasant drive home.

End of Diary

Report in Herefordshire Newspaper – 1967

MISS CHAVE CELEBRATES HER 100TH BIRTHDAY!

In the 17th century house known as The Moor, Hereford, in its green oasis of fields and garden behind Widemarsh Common, Miss Florence M. Chave celebrated her 100th birthday on Sunday.

Slim and upright and with the quiet dignity for which she is so highly respected in Hereford, she received numerous relatives and friends, including the Mayor and Mayoress of Hereford, on Sunday morning. She also took a long-distance telephone call from Australia where she has a number of relatives to whom she writes frequently.

Miss Chave's father, Mr W F Chave, bought the cider firm of William Evans & Co. Ltd, which had premises near Widemarsh Common. Mr Chave, who was Mayor of Hereford in 1891, made the Evans cider firm into one of the most progressive in the country. He early recognised the importance of scientific work, and an up-to-date laboratory was erected in Hereford in 1900. A new factory was also opened in Devonshire.

The firm was later run by Miss Chave's brother, the late Mr E W H Chave, her cousin the late Mr E Bond, and the late Mr W R Bufton. It was from the Evans cider laboratories that pectin manufacture was pioneered in this country.

The fine old house, The Moor, which adjoined the cider factory, is dated 1640 and has Stuart, Queen Anne and Georgian features. Few houses in the county are run today so graciously as Miss Chave runs The Moor.

The Moor House, Hereford
Photo: Carol Parker

Two gardeners keep the charming garden as neat as it has always been. A cowman looks after the three Jerseys which browse contentedly in the field beyond the garden gate. Butter for the household's need is hand churned in the dairy as it has been from Victorian times.

Miss Chave's grandparents on both her father and mother's side were Devonshire farmers, and it is a tradition at The Moor that home-made Devonshire cream is served for tea.

Miss Chave, who retains such a remarkable spirit of agelessness, paid a warm tribute to her companion, Miss Nell Martin, and her cook, Miss Edith Williams, on her birthday. They have been with her many years, and Miss Chave said: "It is to their care that I must attribute much of my health and happiness."

"Indeed, I have had a happy life and I am never dull. There is always plenty to keep me interested."

An unusual quality of contentment in Miss Chave is admired by her close friends and relations. A cousin, Mrs Lucy Matthews, of Bartonsham Farm, said: "Miss Chave is remarkable because she never talks about the 'good old days', and I like her for it. She is so 'with it' and knows everything that is going on in the country and in the world. She keeps in close touch with her family".

But the good old days were good for Miss Chave. She admitted it on her birthday. "But good things have come, too, in modern times," she said with a smile, "particularly the benefit of being able to keep a warm house. There is no doubt that we had far colder winters in the last century, and our houses were very cold indeed."

Miss Chave has always been a great lover of home, and, indeed, was the daughter who stayed at home and ran The Moor from early womanhood. She had two sisters and three brothers.

But she travelled, too. There have been three visits to Australia. Her father had to keep an eye on a sheep station for a member of the family and the first trip was before the turn of the century. Miss Chave thinks that this sheep station is unique. On its campus live her nieces and their families, all occupying different houses, so that it is a remarkable family concern.

Miss Chave always returned home contentedly from her journeys to Australia and continued to manage her household so skilfully.

At the age of 100, she rises at 8 a.m. and goes to bed at about 11 p.m. Her favourite room in the house is a small sitting room overlooking a secluded corner of the garden, full of flowers. It is used as a study because much of Miss Chave's time is spent reading newspapers and periodicals and writing letters. She studies the Stock Market closely and is said to be a wizard with stocks and shares.

She remembers in 1967 the cold winters when skating on the Wye and at Huntington Pool were enjoyed nearly every year. The snow would often be nearly as high as the house. She remembers how she and her brothers and sisters loved to visit the cider factory and eat cones of sugar which were piled up ready to sweeten the rough cider, which farmers made on the farms and sent to the factory in Victorian days.

She remembers her schooldays at Hereford Ladies College a Victorian establishment in one of the tall houses between Maylord Street and Blueschool Street. For physical recreation they played rounders. Miss Chave doesn't think she missed anything by being a schoolgirl before hearty games of hockey came in. Violent physical exercise never appealed. She has a quiet laugh when she tells her friends that it certainly isn't fresh air which has

Miss Chave with nieces, Prellie and Peg, 1958
[Courtesy of Sally McLean]

kept her so healthy as a centenarian. She has never slept with her bedroom window wide open. She likes it firmly closed at night. But she has been a spartan for cold water bathing and washing. She cultivated the habit in Australia long ago. Miss Chave has always liked young people, and it was a custom in the old days for all the children of the family to have tea at The Moor on Christmas Day. Miss Chave has always kept a large dog and it would be trained to carry round a basket of gifts for the children.

For over 40 years Miss Chave has been subscribing to the Hereford Lads' Club built on ground originally belonging to the Moor House.

She is a member of Huntington Women's Institute and entertains the WI in her garden every summer.

It is impossible to go through life for a century without troubles as well as happiness, but Miss Chave possesses a serenity and a faith which are increasingly rare in these days. The peaceful life at The Moor is like an oasis in a delirious modern age.

THE STONE/CHAVE FAMILY TREE

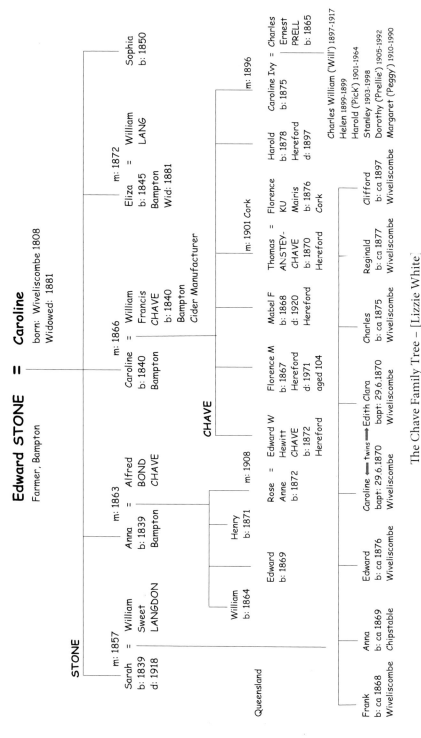

The Chave Family Tree – [Lizzie White]

THE BOILARD/McCUTCHAN FAMILY TREE

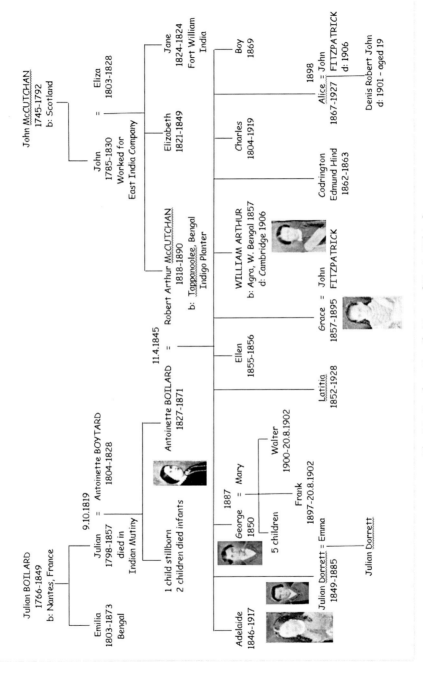

The McCutchan Family Tree – [Lizzie White]

APPENDIX A

The Story of Mac and Flo

A young Anglo-Indian of French/Scottish extraction, William Arthur McCutchan (known affectionately as 'Mac') arrived in the Somerset village of Stoke sub Hamdon in 1890. He had been studying in Edinburgh to become a doctor when his brother, Julian, died suddenly in India. Julian had been paying for his medical studies, and so Mac was obliged to find himself paid work as a medical assistant in order to continue his course. He spent four years working for Dr Walter Winter Walter, lodging at his home, 'The Gables.'

At the beginning of 1895, Mac, having qualified as a doctor, left Stoke sub Hamdon and took up the position of Assistant Medical Officer in Burghill Mental Asylum, just outside Hereford. It was in Hereford that he fell in love with Florence Chave. Her announcement that she was engaged to a penniless Anglo-Indian working in a lunatic asylum was received by her family with a degree of anxiety which encouraged Flo to keep her engagement secret from the outside world.

Meanwhile, Mac was doing his utmost to succeed in his career so that he could afford to keep Flo in the manner to which she was accustomed. It was not easy for an Anglo-Indian with no money or connections to climb the ladder in the world of medicine, but after several unsuccessful applications, 'Mac' eventually gained a post as Senior Assistant Medical Officer in Fulbourn Mental Asylum just outside Cambridge. It was a step up for him but he would be a long way away from Hereford and Flo.

In 1905 there was an outbreak of typhoid in Fulbourn Asylum. The Medical Superintendent caught the disease and Mac was left with sole responsibility for running the asylum. When it was all over, he was greatly praised by those in authority for how he had coped with the crisis, but the strain ruined his health and he became seriously ill the following winter. Flo's brother, Tom (who, according to Flo in her diary, had been dubious about 'Mac' initially) left his medical practice in Cardiff and went to Fulbourn to take care of him. 'Mac' rallied, but had a relapse in the spring. Sadly, he died on 9th June 1906, aged 47, leaving Flo £326. 9s 4d and all his effects. His books and papers, together with nearly 1000 glass plate negatives, were found in the attic of Moor House when Flo died in 1971.

Two men clearing the Moor House attic also found a tin containing letters together with a note saying these were to be burned unread on Miss Chave's death. The men did as instructed and threw the tin of letters onto a bonfire. Were these letters from Mac to Flo or the other way around? We will never know.

Mac emerges from Flo's diary and letters of people who knew him as a man who was knowledgeable about the natural world, enjoyed music and amateur dramatics, had a good sense of humour and above all was thoughtful and kind in his treatment of mental patients. Flo Chave was deeply attached to her family, with a wide social circle and many interests. At a time when most women were strictly chaperoned, she thought nothing of cycling from Devon to Bristol. In her diary, she is seldom downhearted, and spends no time bemoaning her lot as the eldest sister looking after her parents. It was tragic that 'Mac' and Flo didn't marry and have children, but perhaps it was Flo's love for 'Mac' and the confidence that his love gave her, which made her into the serene, contented woman of the newspaper report of 1967.

The Finding of Mac's Photos and Flo's Diary

Dr McCutchan's photographs of Stoke sub Hamdon and its people have been used for over 20 years in local history exhibitions and as illustrations for books. The village is lucky to have such a fascinating record of life in the area in the 1890s.

These photographs would have been lost had it not been for Mr John Soulsby who rescued them from the Moor House upon the death of Florence Chave in 1971. One thousand glass plate negatives had been stored in the attic of Moor House. Possibly Mac left these with Flo when he moved from Hereford to Cambridge in 1902, or perhaps they were amongst his effects which she inherited when he died in 1906. Mr Soulsby sent 500 of these glass plate negatives to Somerset Record Office in 1971.

Group of unknown youngsters at Stoke sub Hamdon – 1890-94
Photo: Dr W A McCutchan

Carol Parker and I (members of Stoke History Group) were intrigued by Mr Soulsby's account of how the glass plate negatives were found, and his theory of the link between Florence and 'Mac' whereby he suggested that the couple never married because the family disapproved of the match. We found in the Hereford Archives' online catalogue mention of a diary written by Flo's sister, Mabel, and so Carol and I went to Hereford in 2019 to look at this and the rest of the family papers held there. Imagine our excitement when we discovered the diary was actually written by Flo herself, and covered the period of her engagement to Mac!

Unknown young woman Stoke sub Hamdon 1890-94.
'Mac' took hundreds of photos – old, young, groups and landscapes –
but he seems to have had an eye for a pretty girl!

Photo: W A McCutchan

From what Flo wrote in her diary, it seems that, although at first doubtful about the match, her parents did not actually forbid the marriage – in fact her father offered to help financially – but the couple were waiting for Mac to progress in his career before marrying. Sadly, he died before this could happen.

There is a postscript to the story of the photographs. Only 500 of the 1,000 glass plate negatives were sent to Somerset by Mr Soulsby in 1971. What happened to the other 500? Carol and I had wondered about this for years.

In the course of my research for the novel about the diary, *You and You Only*, I was exceedingly fortunate to find Elizabeth Semper O'Keefe, once the archivist at Hereford Archives, and fellow Chave family enthusiast. In addition to all the help she gave me in my research, she put me in touch with a local photographer, Mr Stuart Webb. Mr Soulsby had been going to throw 500 of the glass negatives away in 1971 as they were mainly

Two unknown little girls – Stoke sub Hamdon 1890-94
Photo: W A McCutchan

Unknown subjects – Stoke sub Hamdon 1890-94 – Not a good photo as one of the children obviously moved, but it shows the easy relationship between photographer and subjects.
Photo: Dr W A McCutchan

portraits of unknown people, but knowing Stuart's interest in Victorian photography, Mr Soulsby passed them on to him. It was due to Stuart that the glass negatives survived.

Stuart was fascinated, not only by the fact that these pictures were beautiful and contained a wealth of information on Victorian life and costume, but, having done a great deal of work on other Victorian photographs where the faces as a rule have very serious expressions, he was struck by the way 'Mac's' subjects were often smiling at the camera, – especially the children – as if they liked him, as if they were sharing a private joke. Stuart felt that the pictures told us a great deal about the photographer.

Stuart very generously gave me all the glass negatives and the prints he had made from them. He said he felt he had been their caretaker all these years and was glad to think that they were going home. My husband, Phil Hodges, took on the mammoth task of scanning all the images from the glass plate negatives onto computer, and it was then discovered just how much the glass plates had deteriorated over the years, in spite of Stuart's careful storage of them. If Stuart had not taken print copies earlier, many of the images would have been lost. The prints will now be scanned, and the glass plate negatives, together with electronic images of both these and the prints, will be sent to the Somerset Heritage Centre in Taunton.

Unknown little boy, Stoke sub Hamdon 1890-94
Photo: W A McCutchan